Robin
On the Out
Nottingham and Sherwood Forest

A companion and tour guide on a
theme of 12th Century 'Robin Hood Country'

by
Richard Rutherford-Moore

author of The 'Legend of Robin Hood'

www.capallbann.co.uk

Robin Hood
On the Outlaw Trail in Nottingham and Sherwood Forest

©2002 Richard Rutherford-Moore

ISBN 186163 184 7

Cover design by Paul Mason

Published by:

Capall Bann Publishing
Freshfields
Chieveley
Berks
RG20 8TF

Richard Rutherford-Moore has been fascinated by history from boyhood. A long-term 'living history' exponent and re-enactor bred both research and practical skills and led to him travelling the world serving behind and in front of camera on television drama serials such as 'Soldiers' (1990) 'Sharpe' (1992-7) and 'Hornblower' (1998-9) as a historical / technical adviser and armourer. Richard's outdoor skills, enthusiasm, affability and easy-going narrative style led to him becoming a historic tour guide in 1994. Dressed as a 12th Century medieval forester, Richard features in recent Nottinghamshire Tourist brochures and presented "Robin Hood's Sherwood Forest" to the academic delegates presenting papers at the 2nd International Robin Hood Studies Convention, held in Nottingham in July 1999. Richard served as the historical consultant to The History Channel USA production, "History Mystery ; The Legend of Robin Hood" and appearing at The MIllenium Dome.

The author would like to thank :

Nottinghamshire Tourist Unit
Nottingham Civic Society
Nottingham Castle Museum and Art Gallery
Nottingham Local Studies Library
Nottinghamshire County Archive
Arnold Library
The Bestwood Country Park Rangers
Graham Black
Margaret Harrison
Tony Rotherham
Aztec (UK) Internet Solutions Ltd
Ian Storer for illustrations

Contents

Introduction by Ye Author

Maps included :
Nottingham, AD1100 - AD1300
Sherwood Forest, circa AD1200

Introduction by ye author and guide

Welcome to Robin Hood Country! This booklet written by 'public demand' is designed to give you a detailed background to some of the places and people to visit and a quick reference to daily affairs in this beautiful Shire during the time of 'Robin Hood'. We follow the theme of Robin Hood through the county; there is - as you will find out - very much more than the marvellous story of the world's most famous outlaw here to see and explore.

As many rreaders will already know I am not a native of this shire, being born further north in what is now South Yorkshire. My boyhood was always accompanied by tales of Robin Hood as I was brought up near Loxley, having a claim as the birthplace of our outlaw hero. I have collected many old Robin Hood storybooks; the magic in their pages has remained with me since those early days. Some folk have in the past - and today - through story and the more modern media of television and cinema, changed the legend of Robin Hood both for good and bad; but his versatility throughout is one of the things that has ensured his continuity. Some of the qualities now attributed to Robin Hood are so unbelievable and unattainable that some people attempt to belittle them instead. You'll spot both aspects - the acknowledgement of his finer qualities and the trivialisation of them - running in close parallel on any visit. You'll probably - if you're still undecided - be able to make a decision as to where to stand in The Legend of Robin Hood at the end of your tour.

I always refer to Robin Hood as a 'hero' although as we will see during the tour, he wasn't *always* the clean-cut, swashbuckling, heroic and romantic merry gentleman we all now know and love. What he stands for today we *do* know, and I hope that when you go away back to your homes you will take a piece of him back with you forever. I wrote the book *'The Legend of Robin Hood'* shortly after I came to live here, following the 'outlaw trail' from my origins in Yorkshire. In Nottinghamshire, he is firmly established above anywhere else - but I do acknowledge the claims and opinions of other counties and the rocky foundations of some claims here. I just found myself closer to the legend in Nottinghamshire than anywhere else.

I used my bicycle - still do - to find the places we will be visiting and explore the ballads and tales of Robin Hood. They were so much more real when you could turn back the history clock - as this book does - and imagine the bushes parting and an outlaw or forester stepping out of the greenery. I tell stories of Robin Hood where they could have 'actually' happened - use people's imagination to try and bring them to life and look for the grain of truth within them; and the echo of them in their modern day experiences.

I also hope - given time and space - to pass onto you the many happy hours I've had poring through the wealth of local history in the local library. You can access over forty books on the library bookshelves if you wish to further your interest in the outlaw known as Robin Hood, and I hope this tour will start you off - or further your existing interests - 'on the outlaw trail'. I've met some wonderful people on the outlaw trail here on foot and bicycle; they too acknowledge the claims and opinions from elsewhere, but as one Blue Badge guide of Nottinghamshire said to me recently, if ever Robin Hood's remains are finally found and no doubt excavated, his bones will have *Nottinghamshire* running through each one, rather like a stick of Blackpool rock. I try never to contend claims or opinions; I hope Robin Hood is happy that his memory is still alive and well, books still being written commemorating his adventures, and seeing people's faces whenever he appears 'in person'. To deny anyone's claim takes him away from what is important - *everyone* helped make him what he is and he subsequently *belongs* to everyone; no matter who, what nationality or where they are. We can perhaps begin our 'outlaw trail' about 35,000 years ago following the last great Ice Age ....

An Origin For 'Robin Hood'

The origins of stories about a 'wild man of the woods', the 'Lord of the Hunt', an 'Oak King' or 'The Green Man' go back thousands of years, way beyond any possible identification with a single person.

In the mists of time, travelling folk who settled here in England from other countries brought their folk-tales with them, and told them to their children around the fireside in cottage or woodland glade. They did not write these things down - tales were transmitted through the oral tradition only. As such, they were never clearly defined in a set form; they changed slightly with each telling. Storytellers used their experiences - and those of others - to illustrate the tales and help them to be understood. The values they were trying to get across have the same underlying themes; they were often carried from one story across into others, with different characters. These hunter-gatherers had a firm tradition of hunting lore; they depended on migratory animals for meat, clothes and utensils. Each spring, season, plant, tree, animal, man, woman and child had a spirit or god in association with them, both good and evil. They sought to weave spells and magic into their stories and dances in temporary stopping-places in cave and forest to please these spirits and gods, find favour with them and ensure continuation through a successful hunt or harvest. Many characters in folklore stories have their origins in these established hunter/gatherer rituals.

In the days leading up to 500BC, there were many migrations of tribal groups before they eventually began to settle down. These people often 'bumped into' other travellers, but it did not mean conflict. Conflict is almost always based on frontiers - of terrain or differing beliefs - in those early days, these simply did not exist. People shared their knowledge, and traded with each other; this sharing extended to story-telling. In time, small tribal settlements became larger. They gave birth to others, linked up or expanded. This more settled existence led to an increase in the esoteric arts of religion and architecture due to an increase in food production through developments in agriculture - the ability to plant crops. Cultures then began to sub-divide into three parts; those who worked to produce food and clothes; those who studied and prayed for the continuity of the fertility of the harvest and the animals everyone depended on by appeasing 'the gods'; and those who fought to defend the former two classes. The tribal migrations settled, established frontiers and the first ideological clashes began. Great states began to evolve - the more successful ones being those who allied a strong military aspect with firm religious beliefs, in order to promote the power of the state, in order to keep and acquire land and expand their territory and status. This led to a growing separation of the warrior and religious aspects as an *elite* status apart from the 'everyday' common folk.

Communications and travel increased; in Europe the first mighty empires were founded on the ruins of Roman rule or fresh conquests, flourished or fell (on the borders and frontiers where these empires touched things were never really quiet). Waves of successive invaders or immigrants to the British Isles from France, Spain, Rome and later Scandinavia and Germany brought their own beliefs, traditions and gods, and they overlapped and intermixed with British ones (*1). Established shrines and places of worship of 'old' gods were simply adopted by any new arrivals and re-dedicated to 'new' ones. Christianity when it arrived in Britain introduced The One God (and a new set of supporting roles in the form of 'saints') but was far less tolerant, absorbing some of the old beliefs but abolishing the majority. For example today, the name of the old Celtic goddess *Eostre* only survived through Christianised Easter; ancient *Samhain* ('Summer's End' / Hallow'een) was also 'Christianised' as All Saints Day, and the pagan festival of *Yule* became Christmas.

The warrior classes began to introvert and develop their own ideas above simply slicing each other up in warfare with edged weapons or blunt instruments and established a code of honour, tournaments and the basic 'rules' of chivalry; the Church - whilst running the everyday affairs of State and also creating some of the most impressive buildings in the Western hemisphere as monuments - assisted warriors in this and helped them find hope and salvation. Pressure began to build also on the common folk going about their everyday tasks; they supported the above two *elite* classes more and more, until both *elites* could not survive without them. In the power vacuum left by the Romans, struggles began to take place in England around AD400 - faced with invasion and another potential take-over - for possession of men's bodies and souls, to tie them in loyalty to the land and a rule of law controlled by these two classes. After all, both of these classes were working very hard - as they saw it - in the best interests of the common man!

The severe 'Forest Law' is traditionally identified with the Norman Conquest, although these laws were established well before this. In the year AD800, woodland still covered around 25% of England. The struggle by people to re-possess what they saw as 'their' forests from what was widely seen as 'oppression' and an infringement of their liberty and rights was going on well before Magna Carta - in which these strict laws were first partly repealed through the 'Charter of the Forests' - through to 1450 which saw the beginning of printed works about 'Robin Hood'. The dark and mystical forest was a natural refuge and the ideal setting with it's ancient superstitions for dissent, outcasts, rebels - and outlaws. Poaching game on estates today - although not as widespread as in our recent past - still has a familiar echo and carries the popular image of a stealthy 'Robin Hood' type-character cocking a snoot at the wealthy by roving the woods at night evading the 'Sheriff' and stealing from the 'Rich' for the benefit of the 'Poor'.

This is generalising somewhat, over many centuries; but in my opinion it forms the foundation for the establishment of the legend of Robin Hood. In the early printed tales beginning in the fourteenth century, Robin begins as an ordinary man - sometimes termed a 'yeoman', although the term has a different meaning then - fighting oppression, graft and slavery but then evolves through spirit and class to finally become a nobleman; the 'working-class hero' around AD1500 got pushed up the social ladder by poets and storytellers. Robin Hood was also by then seen to be a firm, decisive, bold and clever leader of men, but he didn't start out this way in the ballads and printed stories; he begins as a rather young hot-headstrong boy who gets into all kinds of trouble through displaying the qualities of youth, dashing in to prove a point using physical means or set an example to his followers perhaps where 'angels and wise men would fear to tread'. Themes of trickery, betrayal, disguise and revenge weave through these stories. Robin doesn't always come out on top even with the help and support of some older and wiser men, who invariably save him from coming to a very sticky end. Nowadays he has almost eclipsed these older and wiser men in the stories and in doing so lost some of his original identity. Why - what took our hero from the warmth of the simple cottage fireside or cave and off along the path which brought him to present day immortality, changing his shape and identity along the way, but surpassing Kings and Gods in popularity? That is what you have to try and find out as we explore on our tour along the 'outlaw trail'. But - studying the legend in detail can be a very lengthy and extremely deep subject. Off we go 'On the Robin Hood Trail' ......

Footnote
1. Near Risingham (Habitancum) on Hadrian's Wall, two ancient stone altars existed dedicated to a Romano-British god named Cocidius Silvanus; both show a tall man hunting with bow and

arrows, a stag and hounds, and oak tree. Sir Walter Scott - already aware of Robin Hood through researching and then writing 'Ivanhoe' - after a visit in 1825 he named the man depicted an 'outlaw' in a short poem; a local tradition at that time named him 'Robin'. He is also connected with Mogons, an ancient Germanic god; Germanic troops served here under Roman control, and rebuilt the small fortress near Risingham about AD208, and possibly a renewed shrine and altar. A local rhyme about 'Robin of Risingham' echoes the traditional Robin Hood story-themes of disguise, betrayal and revenge. Both altars have since been removed from their original sites for safe keeping.

Nottinghamshire has both outstanding natural beauty and many historic sites and you can't possibly see everything there is in the county during a short visit. Collect the tourist information leaflets as you travel for future reference - they give good information for planning future visits; both Nottinghamshire and Nottingham Tourist Information will be happy to supply you with more details. The 'Sherwood Forester' bus and the 'Robin Hood Line' train can help get you around. A few helpful telephone numbers and contacts for planning a future trips are listed at the end of this publication.

Part One

Ye Olde Nottynghame Towne

The Romans in Britain used a paved ford to cross the Trent at Littleborough and evidence suggests they also may have built a bridge at Cromwell, both places between Newark and Gainsborough serving their important road , the 'Fosse Way'. Later, Nottingham was an important site near here linking the old British kingdom of Mercia with the new kingdom of the Middle Angles, first founded around AD500. Nottingham had a previous occupation and name - *Tigguocobauc* - meaning 'cave dwellings' - which had almost been forgotten along with the Britons once living here, perhaps attacked or moved on by the Romans after Boudicca's rebellion (*1). The River Trent proved - then as now - to be an ideal highway through grand countryside for waterborn visitors and the new arrivals decided to settle here on a low hill, naming it *Snotengaham*. Nottinghamshire - then part of the old kingdom of Mercia - changed hands a few more times; at least two major skirmishes were fought between the competing Anglo-Saxon kings of Mercia and Northumbria around AD600 - and later by both against the invading Danish contenders for possession of the hill on the plain below the Saxon town towards the River Trent around 868, finally ending with defeat and the Danes moving in in 877. Edward the Elder (the son of Alfred the Great), with the help of other local leaders, pushed out the Danes in 918; he ordered new fortifications built on St Mary's Hill and also built the first wooden bridge (on stone piers) over the nearby River Trent here in 920, with a small fort protecting the southern end. The town was one of the important 'Five Boroughs' of the Danelaw, before becoming 'English' again after King Cnut died in 1035.

The old Saxon-Danish town has disappeared, but you can find traces of the old fortified Anglo-Saxon burgh by walking up from Hollowstone - possibly the oldest street in the city - and St Mary's Church and around the Lace Market to Weekday Cross, and the later Danish occupation particularly in streets named "—gate". Echoing these old memories, we still use many old names and traditions from this period; the Anglo-Saxon names for the days of the week, and the Roman names for the months of the year for example. Many county villages with names ending in -ham, -ton, -thorp, -wick, -worth and -ing also echo the days of Scandinavian occupation. Nottingham slowly expanded due to its important location on the road to the important city of York and the River Trent crossing, giving birth to another nearby settlement at Sneinton. The town then expanded more quickly and strategically from the Norman Conquest onwards and particularly after receiving its Charter in 1155 from Henry II (possibly as an apology of sorts for him previously burning the town - see *Part Two*) who also replaced the old wooden Trent Bridge in 1156 with a more permanent one of stone; a chapel also stood in the middle of the bridge manned by two priests who conducted marriages there. The new Trent Bridge still had periodic collapses through the next three centuries due to large trees and other floodwater debris surging down the river and colliding with its arches (*2).

Compared to the larger towns like London or York, towns like Nottingham at this time might have an average population of around five to nine hundred persons, rising to over three thousand by the end of the 14th Century before the decimation by 'The Black Death'. The old term for the Kings' administrative representative, the *shire-reeve* became 'Sheriff', and he lived not in the castle but in a house in the town (in modern Angel Row) named The Red Lodge. The main Market Square of Nottingham was originally divided in two in 1068 by a wall to keep Saxon burgh and new Norman town apart, but it slowly fell into disuse and was demolished throughout the next century. Robin Hood performed feats of archery here in the Market Square in two old stories 'Robin Hood and the Potter' and the 'lytell Geste'. St Mary's Church on the Saxon hill (now The Lace Market) serves as one of the settings for the story of 'Robin and the Monk'; the famous and ancient tavern now named *The Tryppe to Jerusalem* in the Brewhouse Yard below the castle rock originally brewed ale for the castle garrison and officials and could well be the site where Robin and his men entertained Royal Foresters in the story 'Robin Hood's Delight'. Will - Stutely, Scathelocke or Scarlet - was possibly rescued from near the site now occupied by the 'six-foot garden gnome' as some Nottingtonians describe the commemorative bronze statue to Robin Hood, and the nearby Castle Gatehouse area could also be the spot where Robin Hood kills the Sheriff in

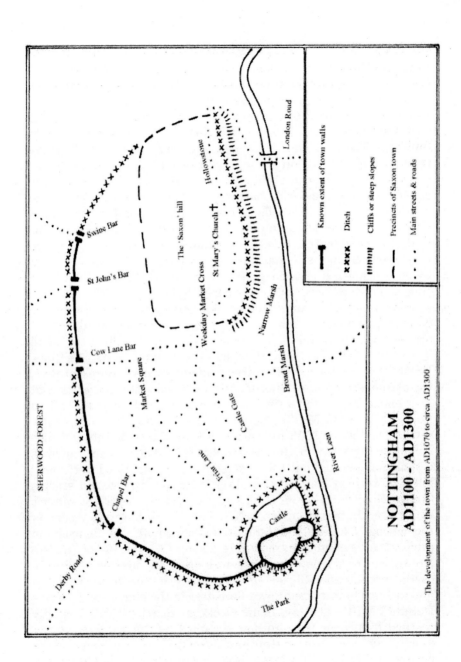

**NOTTINGHAM
AD1100 - AD1300**

The development of the town from AD1070 to circa AD1300

Legend:
- Known extent of town walls
- Ditch
- Cliffs or steep slopes
- Precincts of Saxon town
- Main streets & roads

Labels on map:
London Road
Hollowstone
The 'Saxon' hill
St Mary's Church
Weekday Market Cross
Narrow Marsh
Swine Bar
St John's Bar
Broad Marsh
Cow Lane Bar
SHERWOOD FOREST
Market Square
Castle Gate
River Leen
Friar Lane
Chapel Bar
Castle
Derby Road
The Park

the 'lytell Geste' story. A Franciscan monastery dating from the early AD1220's (the old district of 'Greyfriars', where the Broadmarsh Centre now stands) could once have been the origin of 'Friar Tuck'. That and the old Narrow Marsh slums are now gone, but both it and the Brewhouse Yard area sitting under the castle rock were once dirty and hostile areas to be caught in after dark as they were the haunt of some rather dubious individuals (*3). Historical maps of the town show little change and a 12th Century Robin Hood magically placed in Nottingham today would have little difficulty in being able to find his way around.

Footnote

1. The digging of caves and tunnels in the soft sandstone of The Bunter Bed under Nottingham by people for living and workspace carried on well into the 19th Century. Many examples of old caves and dwellings still remain in situ.
2. The remaining arches of the old Trent Bridge can still be seen, lying partly hidden in the centre of a traffic island near the site of the present bridge.
3. The haunt in a later century of another famous outlaw, 'Dick Turpin'. An early law passed here by the Normans established a curfew in the town (from the French *couvre-feu*, meaning 'cover the fire'). No-one was allowed to be out on the streets after 8 o'clock in winter, or 9 o'clock in the summer; anyone caught without a very good reason out in the town after these times would be arrested and locked up by the Town Watch. It was intended to prevent fires spreading to thatched roofs - and make the 'Saxons' go to bed early to work the harder next day (and preventing any covert meetings promoting insurrection under the cover of night).

The old town walls and ditches of the Norman borough are now gone; but you can cycle or walk around the town using the map in this book and see from the existing topography and streets where they once stood. The town walls may never have fully encircled Nottingham as great use was made of the steep cliffs and slopes, particularly to the south, east and west (see map). Any view into the developing town from the high northern hill outside the walls might have been difficult in early times due to trees growing there, but no doubt these were gradually reduced from AD800 onwards. Seen from the south after 1070, the town with its lofty castle and the natural moat of the River Leen running at its base through open fields would have looked spectacular. The River Leen beneath the castle has almost disappeared; the main waterway there today is the Nottingham Canal.

Use your eyes whilst 'on the outlaw trail' in the town - our Hero can be seen in various guises at spots all over the city; from a 'Robin Hood' inter-city express train, a double-decker 'Park and Ride' bus passing through the Market Square, the famous 'Robin Hood' municipal dustcart complete with 'Merry Men', and in the numerous names of roads, shops and restaurants. The Lord Mayor and Sheriff of Nottingham's limousines are 'lincoln-green' rather than the usual glossy black; and the interior of the dome of the Council House (built in the early 1920's) in the Market Square - nicknamed 'Slab Square' for obvious reasons by locals - has Robin Hood shooting a longbow inside on one of the four panels depicting famous scenes in the city's history. The great bell that booms out the hour here from the Council House belfry is named 'Little John'. The famous bronze statue of Robin Hood (1949) stands just below the Castle gatehouse. The historic St Mary's Church in the Lace Market (featured in the old ballad 'Robin Hood and the Monk') is generally open but you should check for a specific visit due to Service times. Nottingham Market Square still sees major civic events and tourist attractions held here throughout the year. A 'tourist trail' marked by informative signboards at various points can be followed at your ease around the city centre.

'The Tales of Robin Hood' with its tourist attraction theme ride, exhibition and banqueting centre with a souvenir shop and snacks in the upstairs cafe is situated on MAid Marion Way just 100 metres from the Castle Gatehouse.

The wellhead of "St.Ann's"
or "Robin Hood's" Well
before it was demolished.
The wellshaft is now under
the car park of a
public house awaiting
developments.

SHEPHERD's RACE or ROBIN HOOD's RACE

The turf maze or
labyrinth near
Robin Hood's Well
before it was ploughed
up around AD1800.

PART TWO

YE CASTLE OF NOTTYNGHAME

From 1066, the Normans introduced castle-building proper to England, developing from the 'pre-fabs' brought over as part of their invasion force and the hasty post-Conquest earthworks of 'motte and bailey' (an enhanced mound with a wooden tower, a defensive area surrounded by a ditch and all enclosed by a stout fence). There were at the time very few stone buildings in England outside of one palace, and cathedrals and churches; the Anglo-Saxon nobles holding their ground mostly in semi-fortified wooden halls sitting behind palisades, earth banks and ditches but still preferring to concentrate and fight battles in the open. Duke William 'The Conqueror' passed through Nottingham in 1068, going north to subdue the rest of his new kingdom, and chose a high crag and hill towering over the vale of the Trent by hundreds of feet upon which to build a stronghold, due west of the 'Saxon' hill and burgh. At first the crag upon which the castle was built was fortified in the established Norman 'motte and bailey' style, one of thirty such strongpoints the senior Norman lords, encouraged by William I, quickly built and garrisoned to secure their hold on England, and these were later increased in number and also strengthened on a more permanent basis using local materials or even stone shipped over from Normandy (*1).

From 1068, Nottingham's sandstone crag was levelled off (add around thirty feet to the top of the exisiting building ; the button on the old flagpole there - shown in old photographs - was close to the original height of the castle rock) and topped with a wooden barracks, storerooms and a high watch tower surrounded by a fence, with the Bailey - the open field below it - surrounded by a palisade of sharpened stakes on a bank atop a deep ditch. The Saxon inhabitants of Nottingham were called upon to furnish the materials for the castle and also to build it under close Norman supervision - and then start building the new town below it in the area now between Market Square and the Castle (*see map*). The woodland west of the castle was turned into a private deerpark and stocked with game for royal hunting purposes. A large meadow to the south, and later one to the north, were both reserved for the castle garrison to graze animals and be available for any future castle expansion.

By the time of Henry I, stone walls were replacing the wooden palisades of the 'motte and bailey' castles, and at Nottingham the Upper and Middle Bailey and the castle buildings began to take on a more robust and permanent look. In 1140 during the civil war between the newly-crowned King Stephen (the nephew of Henry I) and the Empress Matilda or Maud (daughter of the former Henry I, then married to a Frenchman, Geoffrey Count of Anjou) Nottingham town was taken and burned by Robert Earl of Gloucester (Matilda's brother) but the castle was not captured, being held stoutly for the King by the formidable William Peverel (*2). In 1141 when the Royal army was defeated and King Stephen taken prisoner at nearby Lincoln, Peverel found Nottingham Castle to be untenable and evacuated it, staying at Lenton Priory (which the Peverel family had founded). However, in 1142 it was retaken for King Stephen by Peverel in a bold enterprise by night - a party of soldiers guided by two millers from the castle flour mills (the grinding wheels powered by the waters of the River Leen flowing at the base of the crag) bravely scaled the castle rock on the south side, surprised the guards and got in. The town was burned again during the ebb and flow of the power struggles in 1153, this time by the Empress' son, the future Henry II. He did not attempt to take the castle as it was too formidable - it was abandoned by the Peverels in 1155 fearing retribution when Stephen and Maud came to an agreement after King Stephen's sons Eustace and Simon both died suddenly in 1153. Maud's son succeeded Stephen and became Henry II. Peverel's lands then went to the notorious and rapacious Randolph, Earl of Chester (who incidentally was shortly afterwards poisoned, suspicion at the time falling on William Peverel and his son, being accused by both the Pope and Henry II of using 'witchcraft' to administer the fatal dose).

Henry II then decided to completely renew Nottingham Castle. In 1171 the Middle Bailey was now enclosed by massive stone walls with a moat crossed by the old drawbridge, and a large square tower forming the new gatehouse for the Lower Bailey. He also built several new buildings including a Great Hall in the Middle Bailey to serve as comfortable accommodation - Henry II

Richard 'Coeur de Lion', leader of the Third Crusade and linked with Robin Hood since 1521. (The statue on Lichfield Cathedral)

wished the castle to be a comfortable palace in addition to being a military stronghold for his frequent visits north. Henry II also repaired and expanded the Royal Hunting Lodges at Bestwood and Clipstone, much favoured by his predecessors, Clipstone being founded around 1130 on the site of an old chapel for hunting 'forays' (*3) into the nearby deer park and forest.

King Richard I The 'Lionheart' also enjoyed Nottingham; he loved to hunt and on his rather infrequent visits to England after his coronation hunted in Sherwood Forest. The former lands of William Peverel around Nottingham had been ceded to his younger brother Prince John - but Nottingham Castle itself was particularly *not* included in the gift. John took no notice of this omission however and occupied the castle, garrisoning it with his own men. Richard after his return to England from The Third Crusade (and subsequent imprisonment) found Prince John had put his own men in most of England's castles, spreading the rumour that Richard was dead. Most strongpoints capitulated when confronted with King Richard, but when Richard arrived in Nottingham in March 1194 to find the castle still closed to him he lost his temper and attacked - with a strong party of men he smashed his way into the wooden gatehouse tower using fire and sword and took the dazed soldiers still alive there prisoner. The Middle Bailey proved too strong for him - Richard had to lay formal siege to it and send for 'engines' to be able to break in, but whilst waiting for their arrival made various threats including wholesale excommunication by the local Bishop of the rest of the castle garrison; the prisoners he hanged near the smouldering ruins of the gatehouse tower as a warning to what would happen to the rest of the garrison when he got inside. The two Castle Constables and their garrison wisely surrendered in the face of Richard's angry threats and were spared. Three days later Prince John was banished to France inside the Great Hall here by his elder brother for trying to usurp the throne in his absence, but at the last minute Richard gave his younger brother John permission to come and go in England as he desired.

The forceful entry of Richard I into Nottingham Castle in 1194 was probably the inspiration for part of Sir Walter Scott's novel, *Ivanhoe*, in which Robin Hood features prominently.

Prince John returned to England in 1199 when Richard I died abroad of blood poisoning (after being struck by a crossbow bolt

King John; with the Sheriff of Nottingham and his underling Sir Guy of
Gisborne - the chief 'bad guy' in the traditional Robin Hood legend, seen here
signing Magna Carta in 1215 which he then tore up the year after in the face
of the barons who made him sign it. King John is traditionally held in history
to hold the position of England's most unpopular monarch - he died at Newark
in Nottinghamshire in 1216, and was later buried in Worcester. (from the
statue on Lichfield Cathedral)

trying to get back the castles across the Channel that his younger brother had carelessly lost) and ruthlessly became King John I of England despite some opposition and being wholly unpopular. As a result Nottingham Castle expanded again, including a new tower in the Upper Bailey, military workshops, stores and armouries, more new palace buildings including an private bathroom for a King who unusually for the period took a bath once a month (whether he needed one or not), a new and stronger Gatehouse by order of King John - remembering what his elder brother did to the previous one - in a much stronger Outer Bailey and also laid down plans for a new Northern Bailey. King John spent a lot of time here in Nottingham, using the castle as one of the major depositories for this cash after 1207 (silver pennies packed in barrels, in batches of £100), hunting and privately enjoying himself away from the many endless foreign wars, church and civil strife that eventually lost him everyone's respect and almost half of his kingdom. In October 1208, the notorious Philip Marc was appointed for the first time High Sheriff of Nottingham (*4), and his brother bercame Constable of the Castle. During one of the recurrent Welsh uprisings, the twenty-eight young boys held hostage at Nottingham Castle to ensure good behaviour by Welsh fathers there were hanged i 1212 on August 14 by the orders of King John and their bodies dangled from the castle walls. It led to a well-known ghost story, and one possible origin of the reputed 'curse' of the castle.

John died at nearby Newark Castle in a midnight thunderstorm after over-indulging himself during a feast - amidst accusations that he'd been poisoned - and after losing his wagon train, all his money and jewels including his crown when retreating from the French invasion during a campaign attempting to put down yet another insurrection due to him repudiating *Magna Carta*, signed the year before. Henry III then came to the throne in 1216 after his father's death and once comfortable, in 1251 enhanced the existing parts of the castle, building more extensive private apartments, richly decorated with stained glass in the windows and wood-panelled walls, with guest rooms and stabling. Between 1252 and 1255, the old wooden stakes of the Outer Bailey were replaced by a high stone 'curtain' wall surrounding the entire site. The High Sheriff of Nottingham and the Constable of the Castle were given responsibility for supervising all this new building. The

A 'motte and bailey' castle

town was also almost encircled by a wooden palisade stuck into a bank atop a deep ditch.

Edward I in his turn used Nottingham Castle as a Midlands powerbase, holding the area when he was away fighting the Scots and Welsh. He ordered rebuilt and refurbished most of the old buildings in the castle and also ordered, some extra strong towers, such as 'Edward's Tower', 'Romylow's Tower' (named after the Constable of the Castle at the time, who supervised the building of the tower) and the 'Black Tower' to be constructed. The Kings' Chapel was re-roofed and extra windows added. One of England's most successful kings, Edward I's territorial gains and strong rule collapsed after his death with the accession of his son, the weak Edward II. Robert the Bruce invaded England soon after the death of Edward I, reaching as far as South Yorkshire. The people of Nottingham themselves rebelled and attacked the Castle in 1315, but were unable to take it after a siege of eight days, the castle being held at the time by a garrison of only thirty men but quite secure behind the new fortifications. Edward II, after successive grumblings and revolts was finally overthrown, imprisoned in Berkeley Castle and murdered there ; power passed into the hands of his murderer, Roger Mortimer, now the Queens lover. Queen Isabella was fond of Nottingham, and during one stay in October 1330 the young and future king Edward III plotted his vengeance in nearby Bestwood Park hunting lodge. Along with the Castle Constable, William de Eland, a party of twenty-four men gained access to the castle by using an old sally-port and secret tunnel coming up from the River Leen and carried Mortimer off from his bed. The top of this tunnel is now known by the popular name of 'Mortimer's Hole' and is said to echo with Queen Isabella's screams as her lover was dragged off down it to imprisonment and his future execution. Isabella herself was imprisoned for life in Castle Rising in Norfolk. Nottingham Castle does not possess 'dungeons' as such, but the large storerooms cut into the castle rock could and did serve as prison cells for some very important people; like David II of Scotland imprisoned by Edward I in 1346, the speaker of the House of Commons by Edward III in 1374, and the entire civic assembly of Lord Mayor, Aldermen and Sheriffs of London by Richard II in 1392!

During the Wars of the Roses, Edward IV and his brother, the future Richard III supervised the last of the buildings at the castle; spacious state apartments with large and beautiful bay windows looking out over the Middle Bailey, and a new tower behind them - the largest ever erected here, a miniature castle in itself - named 'Richard's Tower'. Richard III raised his flag here to rally an army to fight Henry Tudor in August 1485 before going off across old Trent Bridge down into Leicestershire and the Bosworth battlefield; after his death there, Nottingham Castle began its slow decline over the next hundred years.

By the time of the first of the English Civil Wars of the 17th century, it was almost in ruins but still served as a strongpoint for holding the town and the Trent Bridge. Charles I raised his standard here to declare war on Parliament in August 1642 at a spot (marked by a plaque) on nearby Standard Hill, but Nottingham responded badly to him and after he left the castle was occupied by his enemies, Parliamentary forces under Colonel Hutchinson. Nearby Newark Castle was held by the Royalists, and several attacks from there tried to capture Nottingham Castle. In January 1644 after a moderate success the preceding autumn, they captured the artillery positions at Trent Bridge, went on to capture the town and pushed the Parliamentary garrison right back into the castle itself. Many of the old church steeples of Nottingham overlooking the castle had been used as vantage points during the earlier attacks; St Nicholas' Church had as a result been pulled down. During an attempt to deliver a letter threatening to burn the town unless the castle surrendered, the Royalists were finally beaten back in furious street fighting in bitter winter weather by a sudden counter-attack from the castle. In 1651, following the surrender of Charles I at nearby Southwell (Colonel Hutchinson was later one of the signatories of the Royal death warrant) Parliament decided to demolish the castle. The local population carried out this work supervised by the military, no doubt happy to have such an excellent 'quarry' for new building stone right inside the town. In 1660 following the Restoration of Charles II, the castle ruins passed into the possession on the Duke of Newcastle, who built the mansion on the rock you can see today, beginning in 1679. The castle rock (under the Upper and Middle Bailey) was lowered to permit a more extensive ground plan for the planned palace and terrace; just above the roof of the present building marks the approximate top of the old castle rock the Normans would have known. The Middle Bailey also lost some of its height and length to form 'The Green', and the southern end moat was deepened beyond retaining walls to give access to the mansion's kitchens, coach house and servant quarters. The Duke never saw the end result of all this building and digging; just before the mansion was finished, he unfortunately died. In October 1831, this impressive but empty building (no-one actually lived there) was gutted by fire, started by the Nottingham mob as a result of the then Duke's opposition to the new Reform Bill resulting in its failure in the House of Commons. The lead roof melted in the terrific heat and a solid stream of the cooled and shiny metal was seen next day stretching all the way down the castle rock to the River Leen.

For the next fifty years, the blackened ruined remains of this once fine mansion stood on the rock, visited only by the drill meetings of the rifle volunteers in the 1860's, the 'Robin Hood Rifles' (a plaque on the south front marks the site of their first parade). In 1875, after the then Duke of Newcastle having turned down previous requests to make it a prison or a law court, then agreed to the refurbishing of the site as the new city museum. It lost its upper floor in the ensuing renovations by a local architect Thomas Chambers Hine (one side was too badly damaged to repair completely, and windows were fitted into the old second floor ceiling to throw more light into the interior galleries). In July 1878

26

Nottingham's new Museum of Fine Art - the first outside London - was opened by the Prince of Wales (later King Edward VII) whilst staying at Bestwood Lodge.

In 1189 an earth tremor was felt in Nottingham (it caused some damage to the front of nearby Lincoln Cathedral, and in local legend caused Grimston village near Ollerton to sink beneath the sod and disappear). Cracks were noticed in the sandstone used in the old castle walls; the poor building quality of these sandstone blocks is the main cause of the 'curse' of Nottingham Castle. The Castle - and the future Ducal mansion - were always found to be cold and draughty, due to their lofty situation being open to bad weather which even today at times still causes some structural damage.

Nottingham Castle, the Duke of Newcastle's palladian-style mansion burns after being set on fire by the mob in October 1831, viewed from The Park district.

Footnotes

1. The formidable fortress of Caen in Normandy was Duke William's capital and stronghold, built in fine stone and finished in 1060. 'Military engineering' in terms of siegecraft had not kept pace with castle building; the reduction of even a small defensive work by an attacking force would mean a prolonged siege. Many commanders did not have the capability to attack these wood or stone castles by assault, tunneling or mining, and most were taken by simply surrounding them and waiting for the garrison inside to starve. This took time; during which the castle inhabitants would

hope to be supported by the concentration of friendly forces to operate outside the walls to 'relieve' it before the castle stores ran out. A castle had to be eliminated and couldn't simply be by-passed by an enemy as the garrison would then *sortie* out and harass the enemy 'rear' and their lines of communication. The introduction of the trebuchet and ballista by the middle of the 12th century introduced the next main phase of castle-building in terms of placing towers in a curtain wall, and the building of a central stone citadel, 'donjon' or 'keep' such as at Conisburgh, north of Nottingham.

2. William Peverel's name today lives on today at Castleton in Derbyshire with the impressively inaccessible castle site known as 'Peverel of the Peak', immortalised by Sir Walter Scott in *Ivanhoe* and now managed by English Heritage. The first William Peverel - the first Constable of Nottingham Castle and first Justice of the Royal Forest of Sherwood - was reckoned at one time to have enjoyed such high favour through being an illegitimate offspring of William the Conqueror.

3. 'Forêt' - the French word for forest, and pronounced 'foray'. Post-1066, it became the legal term for the area encompassed by a boundary and being the sole preserve of the Crown for both hunting, timber and agricultural revenue (for more detail see Part Four).

4. One of the more distasteful foreign officials placed in positions of power by King John, named by the Barons in *Magna Carta* as one of the persons they would like the King to get rid of. The Marc brothers - Philip, Reginald and Peter - wielded great power in the county of Nottinghamshire after John's accession to the throne. The ruthless Philip nevertheless remained King John's most steadfast friend, confidant and advisor after all others had deserted him.

Nottingham Castle features in the Robin Hood ballads, notably the earliest printed story of 'Robin Hood and the Monk', and of course in the famous 'lytell Geste'. The proud castle here stoutly served for five hundred years as a solid declaration of the power of the State. The castle served as the most prominent provincial base north of London until well into the fifteenth century, but by the end of the century it had 'peaked' in power. A fine model of the castle circa 1500 is in the Museum as part of the History of Nottingham permanent exhibition, and is well worth a visit. Standing today in the Park or on Canal Street and looking up can still give a good impression of what a formidable sight the old castle must have been, dominating the landscape to the south for miles. You can trace the large Northern Bailey and get some extra 'worms-eye' views of the castle walls and cliffs going by Lenton Road (the old 'middle moat') which cuts through the old Outer Bailey to The Park, although it is now mostly covered with modern buildings. To circumvate the old Northern Bailey, use the impressive Park Tunnel to reach Derby Road; return by The Ropewalk from Canning Circus to Standard Hill and back to the Castle Gatehouse, now rebuilt and restored in the 'spirit of the original'. If you require a much longer walk, the 'Robin Hood Way', a modern long-distance footpath through the county, begins at the Castle Gatehouse (see plaque there). The Castle souvenir and book shop are in the reception hall of the Castle Museum, but The Nottingham Civic Society also have an excellent shop in the north tower of the Castle Gatehouse. The modern Sheriff of Nottingham uses the south tower of the Gatehouse at varying times for meeting members of the public. New illustrated boards here courtesy of the Nottingham Civic Society show the evolution of the Castle from its initial Norman construction through to the 20th Century. Admission to the Castle grounds is free during weekdays (you can still pop a donation into the box) but a small admission charge is made at weekends and Bank Holidays. There is also a small charge for the unique guided cave tours going deep inside the Castle Rock; there is as an alternative for those small children unable to navigate the steep steps and semi-darkness of the caves in the form of a playground and sandpit on the Middle Bailey or 'Castle Green' and for the more mature visitor an ice-cream van and a tea-room inside the museum. The Robin Hood Pageant is held here in the Autumn. Don't miss the Brewhouse Yard Museum, the Lace Centre, Costume Museum and all the other sites surrounding the Castle; the Castle Museum also houses the Regimental Museum of the Worcester and Sherwood Foresters Regiment.

A plan to rebuild part of Nottingham Castle in it's medieval glory is currently 'on-going'. The nearby Broadmarsh Caves opened up for visitors during building of the modern indoor shopping mall are worth a visit, illustrating Nottingham's semi-troglodyte past. There are many other excellent man-made caves in the city but many are *private property. The old "Robin Hood's Well" in St Ann's where the 'Brotherhood of Robin Hood' once held sway still lies under tarmac in a public house back yard, awaiting the funding to re-open it; the large earth maze once named "Robin Hood's Race" has disappeared, recalled only in the name of a nearby filling station. An evening 'ghost tour' of the city centre can be booked at Nottingham City Information or 'The Salutation' Inn on Maid Marian Way. Three multi-storey car parks are situated near the castle; or save time and money at busy times by using the 'Park and Ride' bus from the Forest, site of Nottingham's famous traditional autumn 'Goose Fair'.*

Part Three

Ye Forest of Sherwood

The boundary of the Royal Forest began immediately to the north of Nottingham where the town walls ended; a plaque in the pedestrian subway near Nottingham's Theatre Royal marks the spot where town walls once stood. Anything beyond there and Goose Gate to the east was *Sciryuda* or *Scryiwude,* the Saxon name for the 'shire wood' - Sherwood - covering almost a quarter of the county in the year 1200. Seen through the rising town woodsmoke by a soldier on watch from the watch-tower on top of the castle rock, the woodland and open heaths of the royal forest would stretch away over hill and dale far beyond the northern horizon.

The late Danish and 'English' kings pre-AD1043 established The Royal Forest Laws initially to limit poaching and predation to extinction and the preservation of game and control potential wholesale deforestation, but indifferently enforced them. By the time of the Norman Conquest, there were over two hundred and ninety settlements in Nottinghamshire (as shown in the Domesday Book) but hardly any in Sherwood Forest itself because of the poor soil content and more amenable sites for settlement around its perimeter. The settlements in the forest itself sprouted up through a growing population mostly in the twelfth and thirteenth centuries. The hamlets established in the forest itself at the time of the Conquest were small with few houses; the forest was a jungle in places and few went forth into these areas unless they had good reason to. Two main communications routes crossing the River Trent ran through it going north to York, one being the old 'Kings Great Way', which the Normans noted at once and built the two strategic castles at first Nottingham and later Newark (giving future prosperity to both places because of this) and a network of smaller 'motte and bailey' strongholds to control it. Coming towards Nottingham from the south, one road crossed the River Trent, passed through Nottingham and went north roughly half a mile west of the present Mansfield Road in the city, passing Linby, Papplewick and Newstead Abbey before turning towards

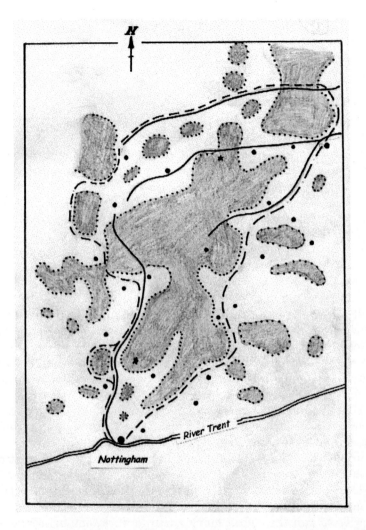

Sherwood Forest, circa 1080. The boundary of the royal forest is established west of the River Trent. The shaded areas are concentrations of woodland, heath and upland moor. At this point in time, open heathland equalled the woodland in volume. Bestwood and Clipstone hunting parks are shown * (Map drawn by the author using information from the Domesday Book)

Mansfield, and then on towards Blyth. The road eventually led towards York, through Doncaster before forking and going northeast and northwest to cross the River Humber at the two crossing-places there. The main road coming north from Leicester beyond Nottingham towards Lincoln crossed the River Trent at Newark and linked up with the former main road just south of Doncaster somewhere around Blyth. All these roads were rough unpaved tracks and as such badly affected by inclement weather ; extremely difficult to negotiate on foot or by horsemen and impassable for any form of wheeled vehicle during or after heavy rain or snow. For long periods in the autumn and winter, they would be deserted because of ice and deep mud until Spring permitted traffic again. Much of the sparse daily traffic were communications between villages, travelling merchants, companies of soldiers, and messages passing between the large religious houses at Worksop, Welbeck, Rufford, Felley, Newstead and Blyth, all carefully watched by the ever-patrolling Foresters. The shipment of wool fleeces by packhorse or mule going to weavers in places like York, Lincoln or Stamford saw a tremendous increase in road traffic through June into August.

The royal forest of Sherwood was administered for the Crown after 1068 by a growing full-time 'army' of bailffs, reeves, foresters, agisters and verderers *(details in Part Four)*. Sherwood Forest was a vast area of woodland, heathland and moor (sometimes referred to as 'waste') and although shrinking from the original establishment on both sides of the River Trent it covered over 100,000 acres when first recorded in 1154, being around twenty-five miles long by twelve miles wide *(see centrefold)*. The original establishment of the forest on 'Yon Side Trent' evolved into three main sections of forest within the boundary (the High Forest, Rumwood and the South Forest) ; these three areas were then split into smaller districts or 'keepings' for more detailed administration and closer control, and each allotted a forester (sometimes referred to as a 'ranger') to patrol. Three deer parks enclosed by wooden palisades or fences existed within Sherwood Forest ; the 'Park', (west of Nottingham Castle), 'Bestwood' (which for a time included Bulwell Forest), and 'Clipstone' further north.

Sherwood was not a completely dense and impenetrable woodland but an area of large woodlands linked by open heath and upland moor, although there were deep and dark places in the

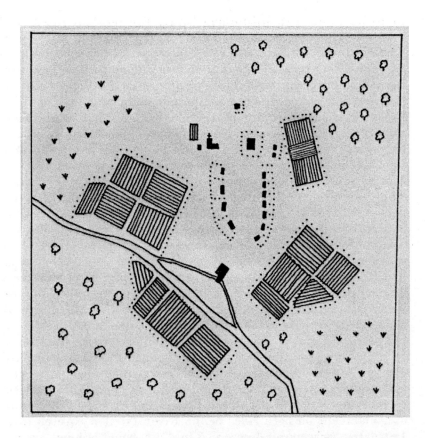

A typical Sherwood Forest village, circa 1150. Crops are planted on a three
year rotation in three fields; alternating wheat, barley and 'fallow'. Each
smaller household has its own small garden adjoining the cottage. The
Manor House lies close to the church and the priest's house and glebe. The
Lord's demesne lies in the fertile meadow, the rest of the meadow provides
good grazing for the village sheep, goats and cows. The nearby woods
provide 'pannage' for the pigs in the form of beech nuts and acrons. The
flour mill belonging to the Lord sits nearby, on the watercourse. The fields
and gardens are enclosed by a stout palisade of hazel wattles or hedges
hopefully preventing escaped coneys or straying deer eating the vegetables
in the gardens or crops in the strips.

trees which folk avoided through native superstitions or a fear of lurking robbers. Areas of open moor and heath were used for hawking after coney, hare or bird with deer chases and wintertime boar hunts in the oak and birch woodlands. Small parcels of Sherwood Forest were let under royal warrant for cash or favours to private landowners, for hunting under these 'rights of warren' or agricultural purposes. There were larger clearings (leys or leas) in the forest due to 'infield and outfield' farming, and also around the old Saxon manor of Maunsfield and hamlets such as Calverton, Linby, Blidworth, Papplewick and Edwinstowe. The regular forest courts with their 'riding judges' granted, recorded and also sorted out the many everyday squabbles, claims and counter-claims concerning the resources of pasture and timber, passing on the serious cases to a higher court (*see also Part Four*).

There were also several 'motte and bailey' castles and fortified manors belonging to the nobility around its edges; the remains of several still exist today - for example at Laxton, the de Caux family seat from 1100 -1300, and one home of the administrative Forest Court; and near Annesley, built in the early 1200's by Reginald Marc (the elder Marc brother Philip being then High Sheriff of Nottingham and Derby).

Powerful religious houses were located in it too, such as Rufford Abbey, Welbeck Abbey and Newstead Priory. Roads - in the medieval sense, depending on the traffic but probably resembling a modern woodland bridleway or footpath - and tracks linked them all; but it took a very clever fellow to know them all and the current seasonal state they were in. As such, Foresters, rangers and local villagers were often sought out as guides by any important parties passing through Sherwood; perhaps supplementing their income by undertaking these tasks (and possibly adding to it again by selling information about the convoy, pack-horse string or a rich merchant to robbers!)

Magna Carta when drawn up by the barons and signed by King John in 1215 included 'The Charter of the Forests', in which a common man's rights to hunt and make use of the resources of forests without undue persecution were outlined. Although revoked by King John the year after, it was the beginning of the end for the royal forest and 'forest law'.

The remains of Rufford Abbey today; to the left, part of the original refectory and 'undercroft'.

Present-day Foresters in Sherwood on the prowl

Little remains of "Robin Hood's Cave", but the nearby "Robin Hood's Seat" where the outlaw was reputed to sit watching traffic on the 'Kings' Great Way' road in the valley below can still be found by going northwest onto the 'Robin Hood Hills', the point of highest elevation in the shire. 'Much the MIller' - one of Robin's gang - could have been an ironworker rather than a flour grinder - an old mill and lakes fed by the River Leen stand in Bestwood village. Another stands in nearby Linby and either could be the possible site of the iron mill shown on the AD1610 strip map of the high road. Linby gets its name from the Anglo-Saxon 'a village near a pool' and popularly claims to be where pancakes were invented to commemorate a village woman whacking Danish invaders over the head with her shallow-pan. From here you can approach Papplewick for a short stop and explore St James Church, the Foresters' graveslabs inside and the ancient yew trees outside; part of the old 'Kings Great Way' road lies nearby. The hand-cut old cave named "Robin Hood's Stables" is also located here. The village of Papplewick, the church and mill were granted to the monks of nearby Newstead Priory by Henry II in 1170.

Another "Robin Hood's Cave" is situated near Rainworth and

A view of the 'Druids' Stone' near Blidworth village; a remnant of the last
great Ice Age and once a dwelling for a family of six.

Walesby, and the Cresswell Crags Visitor Centre near Cuckney - the caves here were used by prehistoric hunters after the last great Ice Age.

The old church at Blidworth is traditionally held to be the burial place of one of Robin Hood's most faithful lieutenants, Will Scarlet. Thomas Leeke, an old but venerable Forester of Sherwood killed in a brawl over a woman, is buried here and his memory marked by a cross. A modern dwelling now stands on the site of the old cottage 'where Maid Marian waited for Robin Hood to come and fetch her to their wedding'. Further west from Blidworth lies Fountain Dale, the site of an ancient Saxon shrine where a retired soldier known as 'The Curtal Friar' is supposed to have faithfully kept the hermitage there for seven years until one day Robin Hood arrived spoiling for a fight; the Friar's military abilities were well-known in Sherwood and Robin - who rarely wore armour - included some in his dress on that occasion! Nearby stands "The Beth Sheppard Stone", scene of a horrific robbery and murder of a young girl in 1817. An old crossing over a brook not far from this spot, once carried a footpath to Mansfield and is one of the places where 'Robin Hood' may have first met his lifelong friend 'Little John'.

The 'Robin Hood Way' public footpath through scenic countryside passes close to all three of the above sites, and a slight detour takes you past the 'Druid Stone' landmark.

An ancient burial mound near an Iron Age hilfort which you can easily spot from the main road was locally nicknamed "Robin Hood's Chamberpot", although the original 'pot' was said to be a nearby stone with a depression that stood by the roadside.

Mansfield was a Saxon manor; a plaque near West Gate, Mansfield is said to mark the centre of old Sherwood Forest. Mansfield has connections with both Little John and Robin's 'nephew, by his sister', Will Gamwell. From there - via The Parliament Oak and Edwin's Cross - to Edwinstowe, the present-day 'mecca' for Robin Hood enthusiasts. St Mary's Church in Edwinstowe dates from after AD632 (the present church was built in 1175) and is said to be where Robin married Marian, commemorated by the bronze statues outside the village library. The church also contains some interesting carved heads and stained glass and also a remnant of an old forest 'land measure'.

A short walk from St Mary's Church past the cricket field and fairground takes you to an ancient area of woodland named

'Birklands' and the Sherwood Forest Visitor Centre via the famous Major Oak. The Visitor Centre houses the 'Robin Hood's Sherwood Forest' and 'Forests of the World' exhibition, souvenir shop, The Forest Table refreshment area and nearby children's playground. Car parking is permitted nearby, and four well-maintained colour-coded footpaths then take you in various directions through the ancient and modern woodlands to suit the time and energy you have (see the guide at the entrance to the Visitor Centre).

Newark Castle on the River Trent - where King John died in October 1216 - has an excellent Visitor Centre, and tours of the castle ruins on foot and the River Trent by boat can be booked there, in addition to a town guide including the historic marketplace. Newark was also the centre of a great siege during the English Civil Wars, and the remains of defensive earthworks and a large fort associated with this period - 'The Queens Sconce' - can also be explored.

Part Four

Ye Foresters of Sherwood

The village of Linby has both a 'Bottom' and a 'Top' stone cross, with the lower said to mark the boundary of the royal forest of Sherwood. Henry II 'aforested' many new areas of England, and the borders of royal forests during his reign encompassed almost 30% of England.

The establishment and maintenance of the Royal Forests by the monarchs of England was disliked by their nobles as it set geographical limits to hunting during any 'chase' (*1); the Church hated the forest laws for the Forest Law Administration's complete disregard of clerical privileges, and their 'inhumanity to Man'; the common folk detested them as they hampered agriculture, and restricted what they saw as their right to hunt wild animals, cut timber for building and gather firewood for cooking and heating.

A measure - it is said - of the strength of a monarch in the early to middle medieval period was how much he managed to prevent encroachment into his Royal Forests by the general opposition to them. During the reign of King Stephen (1135-1154) many incursions were made into the Royal Forest of Sherwood by rapacious noble and starving commoner alike during the civil wars in England between Stephen's supporters and those of the daughter of Henry I, the 'Empress Maud' or Matilda. These eventually led to later major investigations by the Crown in 1170 and 1194 into the corruption of royal officials - including Forest Justices and Sheriffs - who were all at the time suspended from duty.

The Foresters in Nottinghamshire were administered by a high-ranking nobleman known as The Justice of the Forest (a title partly hereditary up to the mid-13th century, each Justice serving for a three-year term) having responsibility to the reigning Monarch for the Royal Forest of Sherwood through the monarch's representative, The High Sheriff. Two of the principal administration centres in the medieval era were at Papplewick in the south and Laxton in the north, both established pre-1135. The Royal Foresters were the everyday 'policemen' of the forest with

A depiction copied from an 11th century original of a Royal Forester at work. The artist has shown the forester taking a hart and a hind with his bow and using swallowtail-headed arrows with carved nocks below the flights. The forester has 'tucked' his *cotte* into his waistbelt to free his upper legs for running, he is wearing a linen or leather coif on his head. The bow is short and stout - probably self-nocked - and note how the artist has placed the bowstring on the wrong side of the left arm. The 'release' is interesting; drawn to the ear? Whatever, the forester's ain is true - he has struck both deer in exactly the right spot and Robin Hood would be proud of him!

the Agisters (responsible for collecting farming rents and licencing the feeding rights of animals like cattle, sheep and pigs at the 'Swanimote'), and Verderers or 'woodwards' (responsible for licencing and regulating the taking of wood and timber at the 'Woodmote') in looking after the area within the boundary of the Royal Forest (*2).

The original 'forest laws' had been laid down by the last Scandinavian ruler, Cnut ; these passed as law through Edward the Confessor and Harold, Earl of Wessex, and were duly 'inherited' by William I in 1066. The strict enforcement of the Royal Forest laws of the post-1066 establishment by William I 'The Conqueror', stated that no-one was permitted to carry weapons, hunt, cut or gather wood for the fire or for building, plant any crops or graze any animals in the area of the Royal Forests without Crown permission in the form of the granting of a licence or warrant as much royal revenue was raised by this system. It meant that it was not just a crime to be in actual possession of stolen game (the origin of the term 'being caught red-handed') but anyone found off the Kings' Road within the bounds of Sherwood Forest carrying a bow, sword, hunting knife, snares, nets or with an 'unlawed' hound in the forest (three toes removed from each foot to make it useless for hunting) would be deemed guilty *by intention* to the poaching of game. The deterrent of severe punishment and the patrolling Foresters were enough, but any trespasser caught breaking these laws had their names taken if they were known locals to be later 'summoned' to court or were taken off and locked up if identity unknown to appear before a Forest Court held every forty-two days in any of the local hamlets. Really serious crimes were dealt with by the 'Assize of Eyre', a larger Court whose Justices visited three times a year, and by the end of the twelfth century a 'General Eyre' visiting every third year.

Punishments were quite severe by modern standards; heavy fines, legal beatings, whippings, blindings or for really serious crimes maiming by the loss of fingers or a whole hand for anyone found guilty - certain incorrigible and hardened individuals caught repeating past crimes could be passed over to a higher court and hanged; but the medieval era was overall a very brutal age to live in, with punishments tending toward violence. Known perpetrators and criminals who could not be found and caught

A Royal Forester on patrol day in, day out, week after week, month after month - needed good stout boots. These are a historical museum-quality reproduction of a pair of medieval boots by English Heritage historical boot and shoe maker, the skilled cordwainer Sarah B Juniper. The author wore these boots on a three day practical historical outdoor trek dressed as 'Blacke Dickon, a medieval Forester' along a section of the 106 mile long 'Robin Hood Way' long-distance public footpath linking both country parks and many beauty spots in Nottinghamshire; another historical fund-raising trek is planned for the near future with the Robin Hood Way Association.

44

(perhaps having escaped from custody) were generally 'outlawed' by the Forest Court and lead to a heavy fine being levied on their home village to pay in lieu unless the criminal was turned in to the authorities by the villagers. From about 1250, the savage corporal punishments of the previous ten decades were replaced by heavier and heavier fines - the Crown being then perpetually short of cash and always seeking sources of extra revenue. Regular 'perambulations' by selected nobles around the perimeter of the forest re-established and advertised the original forest boundary. During his reign, King John always sought to expand the Sherwood Forest boundary particularly to the west and east to gain extra revenue ; in 1204 John sold the entire royal forest areas in Devon and Cornwall. His son Henry III 'aforested' for a time in 1232 a large area to the east of Sherwood towards the Trent.

Barnsdale - woodlands on the main road to York further north - were not part of a royal forest and hence were not patrolled by Royal Foresters ; this area became notorious for the growing prescence of a large number of 'outlaws' and robbers, requiring by the time of the early 14th Century a large armed escort to be able to pass unmolested. Roads there were supposed to be kept clear or undergrowth and buildings for 'a bowshot' either side so robbers couldn't lurk in wait for a passing traveller. Large numbers of common people sheltered in fear in Sherwood and other forests in 1075-6 as William I's soldiers came north to crush the Saxon revolt around York and their numbers were subsequently augmented as the soldiers then deliberately laid waste to a vast swathe of land. Many of these people died unknown, unshriven and unburied.

The Foresters main concern - along with preventing the stealing of timber and firewood and the unlicensed grazing of animals - would be to control poaching and to look to the safe keeping of all the woodland game and fish. They would count and record gamebirds and pigeon, boar, deer, coneys and hares; they would also control predators such as bears, wolves and foxes, foulmarts, martens and wildcats. Regarding the Kings' deer (the oft-quoted 'free-lunch' of Robin Hood and his band) they would report their numbers and whereabouts and help maintain a written record - known as 'harbouring' - of the 'warrantable beasts' (stags five years old or more in the deer herds) and also where they were likely to be grazing at any one time. They maintained a suitable environment for deer breeding, then collected the financial resource of discarded antlers in March or April for use in their many applications. In October they would attend the deer during the 'rutting season', and ensure there were no undue disturbances from predators, animal and human. This done, the male stags (also known as 'bucks' or 'harts', the females as 'does' or 'hinds') would leave their harems and live in groups apart from the hinds and the Foresters would then use their bows to cull older stags and hinds no longer capable of breeding ; a Monarch would use these animals sometimes as a gift to a loyal noble or to curry favour with a high-ranking clergyman.

In May and June the hinds and does would give birth to their fauns, and the Foresters would ensure plenty of green vegetation (called 'vert') was available for both feeding and seclusion and that hind and faun were not disturbed when taking advantage of it. In addition to the native Red deer, the Normans imported Fallow deer and the beautiful but smaller Roe deer lived close alongside, were hunted and hence also cared for by the Foresters. The Foresters kept hounds such as brachets, lymers and alaunts both for the hunt and to single out the 'warrantable' stags; these looked very similar to bassets, beagles, bloodhounds and lurchers seen at field sports events today. Larger animals - wolfhounds, complete with spiked collars for throat protection against a savage wolf - had an obvious use, though wolves were controlled mainly by digging large pits with sharp stakes in the bottom of them before winter, baiting a trap or lying in wait above a tethered lamb or goat and simply shooting them on sight with broadheaded arrows (*3). Foresters used bows for work duties rather than law enforcement; initially they were probably the short and powerful 'Saxon' flat bows or light hunting crossbows but Foresters no doubt kept track of developments in archery and no doubt knew of the simplistic penetration power and longer range of the longbow, originating in the mountains of Wales and further developed on the plains and in the woods of Cheshire. Arrowheads carried by Foresters varied from bird-killing 'blunts', full flesh-cutting 'broadheads' or 'swallowtails' or perhaps one or two piercing long or short 'bodkin-points', all purposely designed to knock over everything from small game like a pigeon or rabbit to a large animal such as a stag, a horse or even a man in mail or later full plate armour. They may not have worn swords very often, but they would have carried axes or heavy work knives - looking like short

46

swords, sometimes named 'falchions' - for slicing and chopping, and following the fashion of the 13th Century possibly a small shield named a 'buckler' if they were expecting serious opposition. They were sharp-eyed, skilled outdoorsmen and trackers, making a fireside home in the forest by night with a few practiced strokes of a small axe and a scrap of blanket or animal hide if out for long periods. They dressed for the season; winter would see them going about their business gloved and wrapped up in a heavy woollen cloak or a hooded 'gardecorps' overcoat with extra leggings or wool wrappings over their single-leg hose. In summer temperatures a plain linen shirt with a lighter woollen 'cotte' thrown over their shoulders, their hose rolled down to their knees and with perhaps a leather jerkin or apron for heavier tasks. Many carried hunting horns or stout whistles for communication in the dense woodland; the hunting-horn music of the *Mort* or the *T'il est Hault* (the origin of the term 'tally-ho') would be very well-known to them.

Foresters were appointed to oversee and police a defined district in the forest by the bailiffs of the Chief Justice. Foresters could request extra labour through the Justice in the name of the King as 'boon work' from any village in the district as required for the heavier tasks of watercourse ('forest law' also encompased lakes, river, stream and brook) and ditch digging or the erection of hunting palisades.

A Forester wore as part of his duties (and so he would be recognised as such) a form of 'livery' and possibly a badge, but a 'lincoln-green' coat and a red or scarlet hood seem to have later become the traditional colours for foresters. A twice-yearly clothing allowance came with the job - grey or brown cloth for winter, green for summer. He was paid a salary of around two to three shillings per month four times a year on the Quarter Days of the 'Old' Style calendar : Lady Day (April 6), Midsummer Day (July 6), Michaelmas Day (Oct 11), Christmas Day (Jan 6), and a bit of land in his district often came with the appointment as Forester for him to grow food.

Foresters gathered to receive their orders from the Chief Justice's bailiffs and reeves at the main sites for forest administration such as Papplewick, Laxton, Linby, Oxton, Mansfield, Edwinstowe or Calverton. They also attended the Forest Courts held in these villages to bear witness for the 'prosecution', and probably in addition were held in readiness to serve as local guides for military expeditions, important persons or convoys heading for these places or passing through the greenwoods.

The Foresters in each district travelled widely each day keeping their sharp eyes open for evidence of thieves and poachers and also keep daily track of the deer, boar, hare and game birds to ensure a plentiful supply of same for any imminent visit by the King for a break from his royal duties in the form of a chase or a hunt. They maintained all the hunting stands, buck-leaps and wolf-pits, palisades and paths used for hunting. Any royal hunt would be arranged, accompanied and administered by these men. Many of them found rich rewards and favour in providing a day of good 'sport' for a world-weary monarch; but they were generally hated by everyone for their ruthless application of the Forest Laws in an era where noblemen, clergyman, townsman, villein or peasant loved to hunt.

From about 1280 the Forest Laws began to lose their stout enforcement and by 1400 the legal and enforcement machinery of the forest laws had relaxed to such a degree they had almost disappeared. Charles I tried briefly to restore them in 1639 to raise much-needed finance, but Sherwood remained ungoverned as a royal preserve until the restoration of Charles II, who like his father also attempted to revive ancient laws, regulations and traditions then largely unknown for over 250 years.

Many Foresters worked alone in their allotted 'keepings' or districts on a daily basis with potential injury or death following close behind in their footsteps. In addition to the hazard of getting lost, breaking a leg in the wilderness, being killed by robbers or

wild beasts, being caught out by exposure to sudden inclement weather conditions, being hated and persecuted by his fellow villagers, the forest was the traditional retreat of the 'outlaw'. Anyone placed 'outside the law' by a continued absence at court or an escape from custody traditionally fled into its dark and dense cover to lie low. It was law for a village to raise the 'hue and cry' after spotting any outlaw or discovering any crime, and they would be fined if not successful in catching the criminal - penalties were extended to any local family or village aiding, abetting, or sheltering a known outlaw, even if guilty of a crime or not, and hence the necessary secrecy surrounding them meant that information was hard to come by. The Sheriffs, constables and bailiffs were in some difficulty due to financial and manpower constraints to police the vastness of the woods and no doubt sought out the assistance of Foresters in doing so. Most outlaws were taken by force rather than through interrogation of family or suspects but after being betrayed for money, being found in their village on a visit or in a weakened state in the woods through unaccustomed outdoor living. The Forest Administration had a vested interest in creating local co-operation and an intelligence facility. Any robber gang or outlaw living in the woods would be disturbing and killing game, lighting fires and probably persecuting the local Forester and villagers - and the financial incentive under 'forest law' of the reward for taking an outlaw (dead or alive) rose from three and a half pennies to ten pennies under Henry II to five shillings during the reign of King John in 1208, the same reward for presenting at a forest court a predatory wolfs' head. January in Sherwood was known as 'wolf-month' as they came in at that time for shelter from bad weather from nearby Derbyshire and Lincolnshire ; one wolf once ran off with a small sleeping child in Linby as the mother collected firewood nearby. By AD1400, there were no more wolves in Sherwood Forest - but due to the vagaries of social, economic and political upheavals there were always numbers of outlaws, who were given the nickname 'wolfsheads' back in Anglo-Saxon times. Another difficulty for Foresters was that some of these outlaws - particularly after an unsuccessful rebellion - were of a military background, armed and also organised - and would fight back if threatened. Elimination of any large predatory robber or outlaw band called for a co-ordinated effort from village informers, forester guides and well-armed men. Single outlaws, robbers or small bands could not be easily found inside a large area of natural cover; they were often probably ignored by necessity until their activities grew so pestiferous as to activate their removal by the authorities or the outlaws made the mistake of bumping into a large party of Foresters or soldiers whilst moving through the woods or visiting a forest village. In that case they would be arrested - if any resistance was shown, they would be taken by force or killed as the Foresters were legally entitled to do.

The foresters didn't have it all their own way. Two felons taken for poaching and locked up near Blidworth were released by an armed gang who during the night broke into the jail, beat up the foresters on duty and then left with their two prisoners. Although their names of both prisoner and gang were known, none were ever arrested or charged as a result of this event.

On occasion, 'forest law' extended beyond the boundary of the royal forest - it was an offence under forest law to drive off the Kings' deer even if they were beyond the forest boundary in your fields eating your crops - if any 'royal' deer was found dead for any reason on your property an inquiry could see you fined by a forest court for it's demise. On one occasion in Sherwood, a deer accidentally drowned in a fish pond which was then named 'deodand' by the court inquiry - 'the instrument responsible for death' - and the pond was then claimed by the Crown.

The ruthless application of these laws saw men paying a bribe for their appointments as foresters and then persecuting the local population to line their pockets, ending up as the often unspoken but everyday enemy of any 'Robin Hood'. But foresters weren't *all* bad characters - many Foresters worked very close to nature and also extremely hard - and when times were equally hard, a piece of meat courtesy of a good-hearted Forester might mysteriously find its way into a village cooking pot. No doubt any local 'outlaws' knew the Bad from the Good forester as they would have spent a good deal of time in close proximity to them on a daily basis (traditionally, it was a forester that rid the land of the wicked and hated William II - 'Rufus' - who recieved an arrow in his chest whilst out hunting).

The travelling, work and time spent in the forest day and night made many foresters old before their time, afflicting them with rheumatism and arthritis; their browned and weatherbeaten faces would - along with their traditional costume and gear - decry the trade of a forester in his prime to any passer-by or onlooker in the market place or village alehouse. Traditionally, Robin Hood lived for over twenty-two years in Sherwood Forest looking like and daily using the traditional tools and gear of the royal forester.

Footnote
1. Not all the area encompassed by the boundaries of a Royal Forest were woodlands. The original boundaries of a Royal Forest having been set were then 'perambulated' at times by elected nobles under the Chief Agister re-asserting them. King John tried to widen the boundaries of Sherwood Forest during his rule - particularly to the east and west - but they weren't 'recognised' by the locals, and caused some upset and unrest (and legal wrangling) and eventually went back to where they were set after Magna Carta. By AD1217, the Royal Forests of England had shrunk greatly through parts of them over the preceding twenty years being granted to the Church, granted to individual nobles to secure loyalty or privately sold off for cash - by then the worst excesses of the forest laws and incursions by rapacious individuals which seem to have taken place throughout the rule of Stephen I, Richard I and John I had been checked. Magna Carta introduced The Charter of the Forests and King John's son, Henry III never managed to get them back in order; in 1232 he ordered a further five thousand acres of land between Nottingham and Newark to be 'aforested' to Sherwood but it didn't last long - this set the precedent for the slow decline in area and administration of the Royal Forests over the next two centuries.
2. The wooden beams in Southwell Minster and the nearby 'Saracens Head' originate in Sherwood Forest oaks.
3. The month of January in medieval Sherwood was known as 'Wolf-Month' due to the animal being denied natural food in heavy winter snowfalls and driven by potential starvation to taking risks by seasonal incursions into forest villages seeking livestock. Records (with some grisly illustrations) exist of medieval attacks by wolves on both village livestock and human occupant - sometimes resulting in children being carried off whilst still alive by these wolfpacks. The much-maligned reputation of the wolf as a savage man-eater and the folk-tale of 'Little Red Riding Hood' have their origins here.

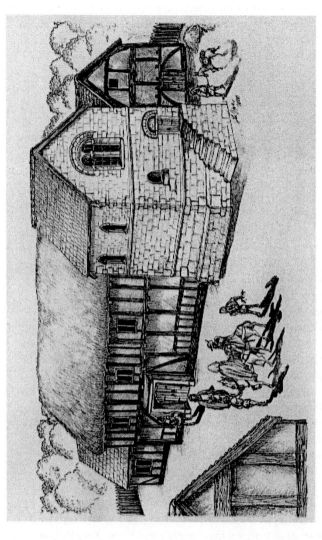

An artist's impression using the author's research of what Bestwood Hunting Lodge may have looked like in the year 1200. The main lodge and its solar and chapel was surrounded by other buildings serving as kitchen, bakery, brewhouse, stables and secondary accommodation for grooms and huntsmen. Clipstone Hunting Lodge was established pre-1130 and later became a 'palace' with regular investment adding a similar 16-foot capacious stone hall, a chapel, tower with solar, offices, kitchen, a jail and a large fishpond enclosed in an area encompassing four square acres. These establishments in Sherwood served not just as a focus for the royal hunt, but also as venues for both open and secret meetings conducting state business. (Drawn by Ian storer)

The old forester districts of Sherwood are now lost to posterity, but many were based from existing villages. Edwinstowe ('Edwin's holy place') gets its name from King Edwin, an Angle converted to Christianity by his wife Ethelburgha, who ruled Northumbria but conquered kingdoms far to the south; a powerful, proud and strong ruler, Edwin was defeated on October 12th AD632 in battle at Hatfield near Warsop by a jealous rival. His headless corpse - his head was carried off to York - and that of his son were brought by faithful attendants back for burial to the spot where St Mary's church now stands. Edwin himself in some Sherwood folk tales is a blend of 'Robin Hood' and 'King Arthur'; Queen Ethelburgha's chaplain and confessor, the priest Paulinus baptised Edwin's subjects in the nearby River Trent as John the Baptist did in the River Jordan before him, is commemorated in stained glass in Southwell Minster.

The Sherwood Forest Visitor Centre and staff of Rangers is a 'mecca' for Robin-hunters as it is situated within an easy twenty-minute walk of Edwinstowe, where Robin and Marian were traditionally married. Many forest paths converge on the Major Oak, traditional campsite of Robin Hood and the Merry Men. The Forest Table restaurant here offers reasonably priced refreshments for all tastes and ages. The highlight of the year here is the Robin Hood Festival, with all the fun of the fair including a market, jousting, archery, sword-fights, minstrels and jugglers, stories of Robin Hood and forest adventures held over a week with a three-day climax over one weekend. Throughout the year, the versatile Forest Rangers hold special days of woodcraft, archery and natural history; many orientated for children. Car parking is free, except during special events when a small charge is made. Wild boar, bears and wolves don't roam free in Sherwood Forest these days; but it is still a home for many kinds of other wild animals, bats and birds. The forest paths are well-marked and if you go quietly early enough in the day (or by night) you will see wildlife in a natural habitat. Please respect their home and the Nature Reserves, always observe the Country Code on any visit, and take your litter home or place it in the bin provided.

'Foresters of Sherwood AD1200' still haunt the purlieus of Sherwood Forest; tours of varying lengths at various times throughout the year by the author highlight their duties within the old Royal Forest, offering a hands-on display of costume, gear and

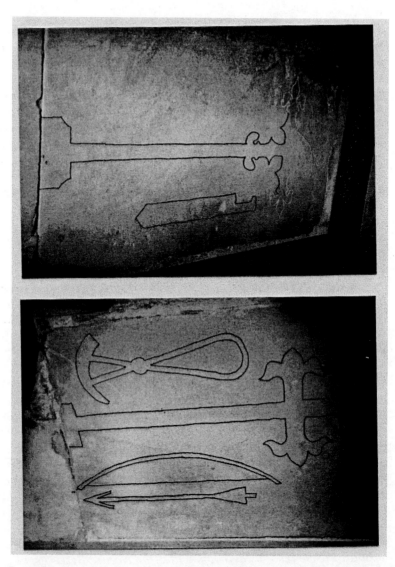

Incised graveslabs in St James', Papplewick; showing along with the Cross foresters' gear in the form of a bow, 'swallowtail' arrow, hunting horn baldric, a heavy work knife.

techniques for visitors and school parties to the green woods by the author including tours into "Robin Hood's Sherwood Forest" (see front cover illustration and end page).

The ruins of the Hunting Lodge and later Palace at nearby Kings' Clipstone can still be seen; situated near one of the three important deer parks in Sherwood Forest. Plans are afoot to fully research this historical site and find out more about it. Not far away from this spot is the Edwin's Cross hermitage and the Parliament Oak.

Charles II gave the Bestwood hunting lodge and deer park to Nell Gwyn as a gift, becoming a residence of the future Duke of St Albans. The area today is now Bestwood Country Park, jointly managed by Gedling Borough Council and Nottinghamshire County Council. 'Bestwood Lodge' is today a modern hotel and restaurant, but retains its antique splendour. As with Sherwood, the Forest Rangers of Bestwood stage events and attractions throughout the year (telephone 0115 9273674 for details). The country park does have areas of outstanding natural beauty and local history; many splendid walks with excellent views enable visitors to take advantage of them. A car park can be found at Bestwood Village following the signs to 'Bestwood Country Park'.

Two early 13th century villeins prepare to break the new ground of an 'assart' in early spring with the new village plough. The iron-sheathed plough is much more efficient than their old wooden one, now drawn by a pair of oxen.

Both men are dressed for a hard days work in cold weather - both ploughmen and 'ox-leader' wear thick head coverings, thick reinforced gloves, lower leg wrappings over their hose and stout footwear. Ploughing will be followed by 'broadcast' sowing, involving wasted seeds and effort.

(An original medieval illustration 'brought to life' by Ian Storer)

Part Five

Ye Forest Manors

We now look at what is usually referred to now as the 'feudal system'. The term 'feudal' is not actually medieval in origin, but it denotes the system of loyalty (or *fealty*) that existed that bound each man through land and a sworn oath to an overlord. The developing unification of England under Cnut and Edward the Confessor pre-1043 led to a fall in outright slavery as the old small and separate perpetually warring kingdoms preceding the Danelaw and English realms had finally disappeared ; under a single monarch and a growing peacetime, nobles found it cheaper in the short-term and more profitable in the long-term to rent out parcels of land to serfs rather than completely maintain them as slaves - such 'emancipation' also found favour with the Church. The feudal system did exist across the Channel in Normandy, but after 1066 was enhanced, more regulated and then re-applied to both Normandy and England.

The *fealty* started at the top and worked down; a senior nobleman would hold land allotted to him by the King in return for allying himself and a fixed amount of men to him in wartime, and in peacetime by enforcing the Kings' will on it (the origin of the term, *land-lord*). The noble would also pay each year a tax levied on him by the King for that land to enable the King to maintain and feed his Court and his personal household troops. This senior nobles would not of course actually work; the rent from his tenants would enable him to buy fresh horses, weapons and armour, spend his time practicing military skills, raising sons as soldiers, and when not practicing or actually fighting, establishing a dynasty or visiting his other properties, by hunting wild animals. His land would be worked by his tenants, who swore an oath of fealty to him in the same way that he swore it to the King; they would receive a portion of the noble's land in return - and the yearly tax-bill - be prepared to fight for him, and they in turn would apportion their share out to sub-tenants under the same terms. These would then 'let' land to freemen and villeins to work in exchange for rent.

So far the system is based on two things; land, and loyalty to the

In an unusual Inn sign, Robin Hood takes a drink from his hunting horn instead of blowing a call on it, after a hard day breaking 'forest law' by felling trees.

owner of it. The advantage is that each man has his place in the system, and knows just what the pecking-order in it is; and in this close-knit community everybody knows everyone else quite well. The disadvantage - of course - is that all the land is all owned by just a privileged few with lots of leisure time and can do just what they like with it! The inefficient semi-democracy and established 'custom of the manor' of Saxon earl and lord slowly disappeared in the aftermath of the Norman Conquest; King William I arranged a vast tally in the form of The Domesday Book to ascertain the actual wealth of his new kingdom down to the last piglet and plough, and administered through a new army of commissioners and clerks got the most from it. There was no appeal to a new tax rate in a system that demanded a seemingly ever-increasing share of it. In time, it led to oppression and injustice for the common man - a serf or peasant could literally own nothing; all that he possessed - 'except his stomach', as one senior Bishop said - was merely 'on loan'.

A forest manor - leaving aside regional variations and using the old Saxon 'book-land' estate of *Anna's Leah* at the edge of Sherwood Forest as an example, where the Saxon lord was dispossessed and the manor taken over and awarded to a Norman knight who fought at Hastings - would be made up as follows. A fortified manor, house or castle - built by the landlord in which to live and give a degree of protection to him and his fellows. A church, storage barns and sheds would be at the centre or hub of the manor (or several smaller manors) with a village (or villages) where the peasants lived. Villages were made up of small wooden 'cottars' with thatch or straw roofs, in which a family lived along with their animals. Each village would be surrounded by three major fields, in which one would be sown with barley, oats or perhaps wheat, and the other field with peas or beans. Each freeman or villein farmed his own strips in each field. The third field would lie 'fallow', used for grazing by the manor cattle, sheep and goats, who would at the same time enrich it with their dung. Each year these fields would 'rotate', and crops would then be planted in the newly ploughed fertilised soil. Any nearby oak or birch wood would supply firewood and timber, and also feed pigs on acorns, mast or beechnuts, named 'pannage'. A common meadow perhaps near a stream or brook would be left alone, used for hay for feeding those animals not slaughtered in the late

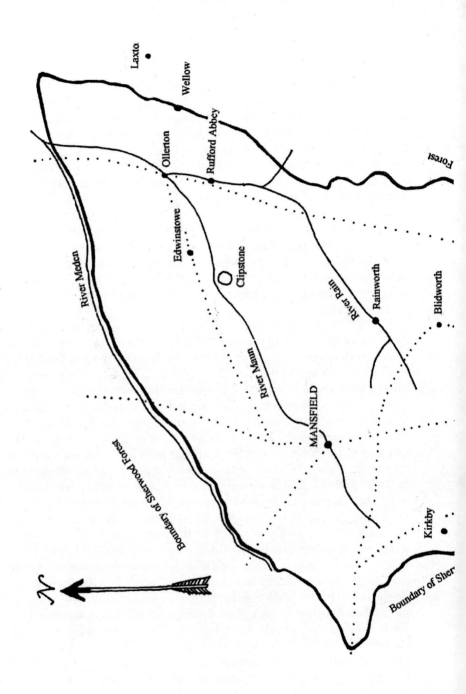

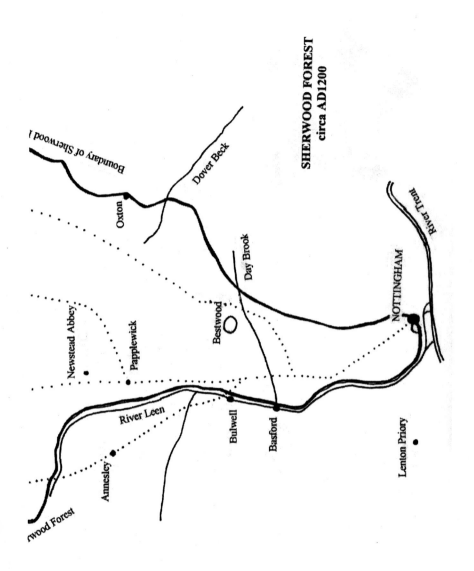

SHERWOOD FOREST
circa AD1200

Boundary of Sherwood
Dover Beck
Oxton
Day Brook
River Trent
NOTTINGHAM
Newstead Abbey
Papplewick
Bestwood
River Leen
Bulwell
Basford
Lenton Priory
Annesley
rwood Forest

autumn through wintertime. A smaller field or fields on the best land - the 'demesne', belonging to the overlord himself - would lie nearby. Each villein would hold a portion of land in each field to farm for himself, but he would also be required to work for around 50% of his time for nothing in the lord's demesne. The land-lord often owned the local mill where the grain was ground, levying a charge in cash or kind and would not permit it ground elsewhere.

The Manor Roll naming those who lived and worked on the estate and from whom and what service was due would be maintained by the landlord's Steward. He would preside in the absence of his lord over the manor court (named the 'halimote', held every two weeks). He would work most of the time at his desk keeping a tally of this return - issuing regular orders to a Bailiff about what was to be done; the Bailiff in turn would issue orders to his underlings, 'reeves' or overseers, who would in turn organise the villeins to set about undertaking the work. There was no appeal to this - at the level of the villein or serf you did what you were told to do and also did it correctly, or you got a warning or even a beating from the reeves who carried a staff or stout stick as a sign of their authority and wouldn't hesitate to use it on any dissenting peasant who complained or couldn't keep his mouth shut given work or during collections from the tally-return. Persistence in any dissent could see a man, woman or child dragged before the manor court and fined or punished until they mended their ways.

A villein or peasant was tied to the Manor in several ways (in case the reader is wondering why they didn't just down tools and move off elsewhere - they'd be rejected by other villagers as vagrants and potential criminals and just be sent or brought back to be heavily fined). In return for his own land in each field, a man would work in the lord's demesne too. He also had to pay his land-rent each year (named a 'tallage', and about a penny an acre, compared with about sevenpence per annum in rent for the land a dwelling stood on in a nearby town). He would be 'expected' to give the landlord a gift at Xmas or Easter too; perhaps a lamb, a goose or pig, a sack of vegetables or a basket of eggs. The overlord could claim at any time a 'boon' in the form of extra gifts, rents or fieldwork. Other required payments were the 'heriot' (the best beast the villein's family owned when the villein died), a 'mortuary fee' (the second-best beast taken by the church), the 'tithe' (one-tenth of the villeins yearly produce, paid direct in kind to the church under pain of excommunication for any laxity) and even a 'relief fee' in any inheritance of land or if any villein took over extra or new lands to work. The villeins were required to have their grain harvest ground in the lord's mill and nowhere else, for which they paid another fee, in cash or kind. If one of the village son's left to become a monk, or if anyone's daughter left the village to marry someone in another village, an extra fee would be levied on the villein to compensate the overlord for the loss of this valuable labour.

Everyone in the village from the reeves 'downwards' worked on the land, or in tasks associated with it. As you can see, there were several folk in purely administrative tasks who required feeding and whom the villeins would also have to support - in addition, the village 'hayward' (a beadle or constable) would patrol the village and make sure nothing was amiss or anyone was skulking off work, collecting any fines levied by the Manor Court for past transgressions; the village priest, who would farm his own small piece of land (the 'glebe') and look after the church tithe barn when not conducting the spiritual education of his congregation. The village blacksmith, carpenter, miller, brewer, shepherd, goatherd, pigboy and birdscarer all had important daily tasks. Some of these tasks called for skilled craftsmen but the less skilful and labour-intensive tasks would be carried out by the village children, who helped out as soon as they were literally able to walk at planting, hay-making and harvest-time.

At the Manor Courts, the overlords could and would mete out their own justice to anyone found guilty of breaking the 'rules'; in some cases, a matter of life or death. Before the Norman Conquest, the Saxon lords levied fines on criminals (named *were-gild* and the origin of the term 'blood-money') in ever-increasing amounts depending on the severity of the crime, and paid to the sufferer of it. Crimes such as murder, treason or arson would not be settled by an exchange of cash, but by the offender being put to death. Duke William after the Norman Conquest abolished the death penalty - to save valuable labour being lost - and replaced it by corporal punishments in the form of fines, whippings, brandings, amputations or blindings with hot irons. His son, Henry I liked the feel of such power over life and death and renewed it upon his accession to the throne ; any crime such as murder or rape, or any theft which was valued at more than one shilling in damages was automatically punishable by death. This power was devolved through the existing legal system onto the barons and senior nobles in the beginnings of a 'common law' to enforce in their Courts - many openly abused it and Henry II in turn tried to curb their power; but it was then too late - many of their savage punishments such as boiling men in oil or flaying them alive were then accepted as 'law'. For example; a man suspected of a crime could be subjected to Trial by Ordeal - if your hand was still blistered after three days after picking up a red-hot iron bar you were judged guilty. A defendant could be tied up and thrown into a pond - if he floated in the water he was guilty; if he sank to the bottom he may have drowned but was judged innocent of the crime. There were other traditions which would seem equally ridiculous or offensive to us today. Many overlords had more unusual rights over their tenants; one was the *Droits de Signeur* in which the bride in any marriage on his land socially 'below' him spent her first wedding night with him, so any child conceived at that time would promote future loyalty through a blood-tie; hardly something today you'd think would endear him to his tenants, but in those days it was accepted and in some places, welcomed and encouraged.

After 1164, a man had to gain his lord's permission to take holy orders and gain his freedom. The King himself would ask for a 'relief fee' for example if a lord's daughter married or if he knighted his son - there were also many other ways of extorting a 'relief' to raise cash that were used by both Crown *and* Church.

The feudal system - although by no means universally employed - gave absolute power to the leading nobles and clergy who enjoyed the benefits from owning ninety-nine point nine percent of England's entire food production. There was no real incentive for the common man to improve his lot by working harder or employing more efficient methods - the system would cream off most of any profit of any increased yield, and unless a 'freeman' a worker could own no land personally. Under a cruel or wicked King, or in the hands of a cruel or wicked overlord, life in 'serfdom' could - and did, even though illegal under the common law - become unbearable, miserable and closely resemble the slavery that true Englishmen - like Robin Hood - despise. If a villein 'ran', he could gain his freedom if he survived by his wits or skill in another town or village for 'a year and a day' - but vagrants such as this were not at all welcome anywhere as they were not governed by the rule of law and usually broke it to sustain themselves, with the resulting fines being passed onto the locals. Only in the former lands of the 'Danelaw' in boroughs such as Nottingham did villeins enjoy the sort of freedom echoed in modern Robin Hood television, feature films and stories. Towns alone saw a rise in 'Freemen' forming trade guilds of skilled workers in the more lucrative trades like precious metals or stones, tailoring, baking and brewing, seeking both to control the vagaries of trade quality and fix market prices and also separate and advance themselves from the rank and file as a 'middle-class' possessing more rare and creative skills than the ones required of a purely physical nature by agricultural labourers who were firmly attached to the land but with no personal stake in it. The modern belief - particularly when featured in the legend of Robin Hood - that before the Norman Conquest the average Anglo-Saxon husbandman tilled the soil as a free man, able to voice an opinion in 'folk-moots', and loyal only to the King himself has no basis in historical fact. By AD1000 the shires of England outside the Danelaw boroughs were largely held by 'aristocratic' nobles under a single monarch with their dependants (tenants, slaves or serfs) working the land under terms similar to that as under Norman rule. The 'English' system was simply inherited and adopted by the Normans but was then much more efficiently and strictly administered, controlled and enforced, particularly after The Domesday Book was compiled in 1086. Before then, the real wealth of the realm was probably unknown. From 1086, ordinary folk in their cottages sitting by the fire watching the smoke curl up and out of a simple hole in the roof, and enduring the stench of human and animal crammed together in close proximity in their crude cottages, would have felt their living standards stationary - or dropping - yearly, particularly with the high monetary inflation between 1205 and 1250. The system was open to many forms of abuse ; approaching poverty could mean a free man and his family might find themselves once again in serfdom. Under these circumstances any bad harvest, civil war, local unrest or a rapacious overlord at any time was crippling - and potentially deadly.

The signing of *Magna Carta* extracted from and signed by King

John in 1215 (a year later he repudiated it) can be seen as the beginning of the end of the system, but *Magna Carta* really only applied to establishing the rights of the Barons and the Church in a Parliament rather than those of commoners. It took the European Black Plague of 1347, the 'Will Cale' Peasants Revolt in France in 1358 and the ensuing 'Wat Tyler' Peasants Revolt in England in 1381 (both these revolts ended badly for both the peasants and townsfolk who took part in them) to begin to really drastically change the 'feudal' system. In one form or another, it lasted into the 18th Century when statutes relating to it were finally repealed but a legacy even applies to the present day in 'tied cottages' and other practices linked to agriculture.

At Laxton (near Ollerton) in Nottinghamshire, the traditional old 'open strip' way of farming still goes on. An excellent visitor centre there explains how the system works, and the village heritage trail is easily followed from there for an excellent country walk.

Part Six

Religion

The word 'monk' derives from an old Greek word meaning 'solitary'. Monks renounced all the pleasures of life, became vegetarians and pledged themselves to celibacy, then cut themselves off from society in hermitages to become closer to God through a life of constant prayer. By the end of the 6th century, this rule had become amended through the writings of Benedict, an Italian monk who although starting as a hermit stated that monks living in solitary confinement were, despite their personal poverty, rather 'selfish, self-centred and indulgent' and should follow Christ's teachings, gather together, and serve the community. Benedict acquired sainthood through founding the first monasteries and by leaving a written guideline as to how monks should live in them; from AD700 until 1100, the Benedictine Order dominated monastic life.

In 1100 there was still a tiny minority of Pagans hanging on with their fingernails from the Dark Ages in the far-flung corners of Europe; but most of the Continent then was Catholic Christian led by the Pope in Rome. Beyond Constantinople in the east and the Pillars of Hercules in the south were Moors, Seljuk Turks and Saracens of the world of Islam. Beyond them and anywhere west of Ireland was completely unknown (although rumour about what was there was rife). Religious devotion and fervour, superstition of witchcraft and even fanaticism was actively encouraged, and eventually led to the bloody, rapacious and disastrous Crusades. Due to religious intolerance anyone not a Christian or not seen to be so was not considered in society, had no say in law or could even be murdered at home or slaughtered overseas wholesale without fear of any retribution; indeed, the clergy through the Pope might give absolution for past sins for doing so. Scientific discovery, medical research, unguarded conversation or dissent from the religious *status quo* could see you denounced and labelled as a heretic and be liable for trial in a church 'consistory court' with the results of being found guilty of a charge of heresy quite severe; for really serious 'crimes' you would be legally tortured until you

A view of present-day St Mary's Chucrh, Edwinstowe. Robin and Marion were traditonally married in the popular legend on the spot marked by the church porch (seen in the photograph) then going off to the nearby forest to celebrate their union. The original Saxon church on the spot marking the final resting place of King Edwin would have been made of wood and wattles. The King Edwin hermitage stood a quarter of a mile away, towards Mansfield. St Mary's Chucrh holds some interesting items, including amongst others the carved stone heads of Henry II and Thomas a Becket, glaring at each other across the nave in enmity for eternity.

'recanted' and even then possibly flayed or burned alive if not banished from the country for life (*1).

You could recognise a cleric by his 'tonsure'; from the 6th Century onwards the Roman Catholic clergy and monks had the top and around the base of their heads shaved and the remaining ring of hair in between symbolised the Crown of Thorns worn by Christ at the Crucifixion. Many new religious houses in England were founded after the Norman Conquest, adding to the ones already here; gradually the senior clergy in England pre-AD1066 were replaced by 'Norman' ones. The state efficiency of Normandy was built on two things; the shock-tactics and individual power of the mailed knight and his company of regular foot-soldiers who could provide the military strength to take, hold and defend land, and the Church which supported them and provided the means of overall administrative control (William the Conqueror's brother Odo was both soldier and a bishop, and any senior cleric was a wealthy and powerful man who mixed religion with politics ; doctrines of both church and state were preached from the pulpit in those days).

In the newly-acquired Norman kingdom - England - the new King, his nobles and mercenaries built not only a network of powerful castles to subdue and control the population but also another network of many strong centres of faith to control 'the hearts and minds of the people' in the form of cathedrals, churches, monasteries, priories and abbeys. In Notting-hamshire, Southwell Minster (*2) developed rapidly into the beautiful cathedral it is today (expanding after 1108 from the small Saxon church and the far older Roman settlement and shrine) but many smaller and more 'approachable' houses were established all around it to ensure the spread and control 'of the hearts and minds' of the people.

The first monastery in this area was at Blyth (Cluniac, 1088) followed by abbeys founded at Lenton (Cluniac, 1109) Worksop (Augustinian, 1123) Thurgarton (Augustinian, 1140) Rufford (Cistercian, 1146) Shelford (Augustinian, 1154) Felley (Augustinian, 1156) Newstead (Augustinian, 1172) Welbeck (Premonstratensian, 1189). There were also Benedictine Orders of monks (St Mary's York, 1086) and Fountains (1132); and then later Franciscan friars (near Broad Marsh, Nottingham, around 1230. The Carthusians finally arrived in 1343, and established themselves at Beauvale Priory.)

Many of these monasteries and houses were founded through the patronage of King and nobles seeking a smooth passage through the pearly gates past St Peter, and held holy relics which often became points of pilgrimage. As a result, the monasteries and churches often vied with each other for these relics, patronage and political power - the Church is still the largest landowner in England today - influence and wealth, despite their vows of poverty and abstinence; high-ranking but corrupt bishops and abbots are the other traditional 'enemies' of Robin Hood through their apparent avarice and greed. Some of the clergy did accept money or gifts in exchange for public absolution for some quite serious crimes committed by members of their congregation; excommunication (used as a last resort) was always a powerful weapon in their hands, and was levelled even at the King and his nobles if they overstepped the mark, as happened with King John (*3).

Monks building their own monestary

Franciscan Friars arrived in England in 1220, and were not based in abbeys or priories. Not being bound to life in an abbey, they went straight to the main centres of population instead of seeking and establishing independent self-sufficient places of solitude as Benedictine or Cistercian monks did and preached the gospel and the word of Christ in the market-place supported only by charity in a belief of absolute poverty. No longer were abbeys the sole centres of teaching, as unbound by their order friars became teachers and teachers became friars, giving rise to the first university schools. Friars were not liked by the established abbeys and monasteries as some of the wandering friars moved into their territory, began to preach and also heard confession; after 1230 many impressionable young men who might have become monks became friars instead, and many young boys were sent to the new colleges and university schools instead of the abbeys. Roger Bacon - eminent scholar and scientist - was a Franciscan friar. Franciscans were then followed by Dominicans (*4).

The Prior makes a ruling in a debate.

Hardly anything remains of Lenton Priory, but we can look at the remains of one of these great centres of religion in Nottinghamshire at Rufford Abbey Country Park. Part of the once great abbey still remains today in ruins, no longer echoing with devotions of white-robed monks and their lay-brothers after a hard days work in the surrounding fields. But - in the maps and models there you can see what it once looked like. In 1086 in the Domesday Book, the area was shown to be merely 'rough land by a ford' farmed by thirty poor souls in eight families ekeing out a meagre existence in the great forest of Sherwood. The landowner, Gilbert de Gant of Yorkshire, had been ordered to burn Pontefract Priory during the civil wars of 1135-1154 and had unfortunately as a result been excommunicated for doing so by the Church; Gilbert was also unfortunately on the losing side and taken prisoner at the battle between the rival forces of King Stephen and the Empress Maud at Lincoln in 1141 where King Stephen's army was defeated, and he was forced to marry the niece of the powerful and rapacious Randolph, Earl of Chester. Both Randolph and Gilbert's father were admirers of the Cistercian Order of monks, quickly growing in prestige since their arrival in England from France in 1128. Other monasterial orders such as the long-established Benedictines - known as the 'black monks' because of the colour of their habits - had been lately criticised for growing too wealthy and employing a horde of servants to do their bidding; the Cistercian Order by comparison was based on the simple austerity of the

'Horn-dancing'; a pagan tradition of dance and story telling
converted to Christianity. (With acknowledgement to the Abbot's
Bromley Horn Dancers)

same Rule of St Benedict - they wore plain undyed white woollen robes and were respected and favoured for their piety, relative poverty and hard work; they were strict vegetarians, they used iron for altar decorations instead of the usual silver or gold, no elaborate vestments were worn and linen replaced silken robes. A Benedictine monastery considered itself independent; a Cistercian monastery saw itself of part of a larger, disciplined Order. Their services, similar to those of the Benedictine Order, were much shorter and simpler allowing more time for private prayer, study and of course - work. Gilbert de Gant chose to seek favour and absolution by 'donating' the land at Rufford in 1144 to the Cistercians in order for them to found a religious house. Gilbert died shortly after the donation was made, and Randolph, Earl of Chester too, by suspected poisoning *(see Part Two)* so the monks had to start with not only working on a poor and windswept site but in addition expecting no support from either founder or patron. The Cistercians had founded Rievaulx Abbey already in North Yorkshire, and as part of the grant a party of twelve monks led by Brother Gamell, their senior, moved down from there to Rufford. A horde of lay-brothers (a practice then peculiar to Cistercians; 'part-time' monks taking simpler monastic vows and attending fewer services) assisted them in their work - most of which in the early days was the clearing of the chosen site for the new abbey and the creation of temporary lodgings for them all to live in and worship whilst it was being built; the rough nature of the site did not appear to put them off at all - rather it was just what the Cistercian monks preferred! The Cistercians as part of their holy life rather liked hardships and also absolute solitude and self-sufficiency from anyone not under holy orders and all other distractions; the nearby villages of Cratley and Grimston were seen by them to be too close for comfort to the new abbey and moves were made to gently 'persuade' the villagers to move elsewhere - moves that were not always successful. Many peasant families at Rufford and nearby Grimston (*5) were moved out at once to Edwinstowe or Wellow, but several villeins resented this enforced rehabilitation. It took the abbey over a hundred years to finally persuade - or harass - them to move to new homes.

By July 1147 the church at the site was complete, and ready to be dedicated. It was named for *St Mary the Virgin* (as all Cistercian houses are still). The building of the church had taken a

An amusing stone carving at Rufford Abbey

high degree of extreme hard work on the part of Brother Gamell who then became the first Abbot of Rufford. The builders did not make the same mistakes as at Nottingham Castle - fine quality stone away from the poor stuff of the Bunter Sandstone Bed was brought from Mansfield by local contractors (along with foodstuffs and other supplies which brought a sudden surge of prosperity to the area, and perhaps also attracting robbers) and worked into blocks on site by the monks supervised by masons fetched up from Nottingham. This prosperity lasted until 1175, when the abbey and associated buildings were also deemed complete. The final layout included dining rooms and dormitories, a hospital for the sick, the cloister, smaller chapels, and a gatehouse with guestrooms complete with stabling for the visitors horses, and a nearby water-mill. Outlying farms ('granges') manned by the lay-brothers grew crops and vegetables and also the main money-earner, sheep; the abbey became very proficient in dealings in the wool-trade. The busy month of June saw sheep-shearing by hand with shears and the fleeces packed into barns on the estate ready for shipment to the merchants of York, Lincoln or Stamford. For 400 years, the abbey existed in an almost unchanged atmosphere of hard work and prayer despite the great changes going on around them. The long-suffering Rufford monks - after work had actually begun on the abbey - enjoyed continuing patronage from the ruling monarchs particularly after 1154, in royal permission to fell trees for timber and clear additional land in Sherwood for expanding their agriculture and grazing. In later years (between 1250-1290) these permissions to change the boundaries of the abbey grounds through continuing expansion were regarded by the abbey as a right rather than as a privilege and the monks did find themselves at odds with both forest authorities and the local villagers leading to a wholesale punch-up on one occasion!

The monks were led by the Abbot (from an older word, meaning 'Father' or 'Shepherd'), who had a *Prior* and perhaps a sub-prior to assist him in managing his flock in a larger monastery. A *Sacristan* looked after the church, with a *Hospitaller* to care for visitors. An *Infirmarium* cared for the sick monks or those villagers or journeying pilgrims coming for help from outside the cloister. A *Precentor* was responsible for caring for books and music. An *Almoner* distributed money to the poor or needy. A *Cellarer* (*6) supervised food, drink, fuel and other living expenses.

The monks spent most of their day in silence - talking was permitted in the monastery only within cloisters, and forbidden in church, refectory and dormitory. However, once outside the precincts of the monastery in the outside world of the *curia* (an outer court and buildings where business with the outside world was conducted) a garrulous monk could chatter away as much as he liked.

The 'choir' monks at Rufford Abbey worked hard at their vocation within an atmosphere of prayer; just after midnight a bell would ring for the first of the eight prayers or 'offices' of the day, 'Matins', which lasted two or three hours. The monks could then return to their dormitories or cells to sleep or doze until daybreak, when a bell would announce the next prayers, 'Lauds' or 'Prime'. In Winter and in the season of Lent the monks recieved one meal a day, but in Summer two meals per day ; extra meals or food named 'pittances' could be granted if they were needed. A light breakfast of bread and ale or watered wine would be served to the monks in a dining-room named the 'refectory' or 'frater' ; all meals would be eaten in silence, with a monk reading to the assembly from the scriptures. In the Chapter House, a meeting around 8 o'clock would be held by the Abbot or Prior after a reading from The Rule of St Benedict to discuss any business arising, correspondence or heavy temporal and spiritual matters and then set the order of work for the day ; any monks requiring punishment would also be dealt with at this meeting. The monks would then walk in meditation or discuss important issues in the covered Cloisters sheltered from rain or bad weather until 10 o'clock when the most important service of the day would begin - The High Mass. Lunch would follow, eaten in silence accompanied by another reading from the Bible or similar holy book; the 'lay-brothers' (illiterate uneducated local men from a poor background not under the same holy orders, who undertook the manual labour tasks and any away from the abbey itself) would eat elsewhere. The afternoon saw 'Terce' and 'Sext' and could then be spent by the monks in 'Collations', or working, gardening, farming, writing, building or fishing, being helped in these duties by the lay-brothers. A senior monk at the same time would instruct the Novices (young boys and men learning to become monks). After 'Nones', another short service, evening prayers - 'Vespers' (*7) - began at dusk, with supper following at perhaps 7 or 8 o'clock. The eighth and last service of the day, 'Compline', began at 9 o'clock. The monks would then go to bed until midnight, when it all began again.

Some medieval monks became learned scholars, and also served socially outside the cloister as politicians, advisers, landowners, counsellors and traders. Monasteries and priories undertook to shelter and feed travellers as part of their creed; royalty, nobility, merchants and pilgrims always took advantage of this, and both Rufford Abbey and nearby Newstead Priory saw many of these dropping in on any journey through Nottinghamshire, sometimes causing the monks worries over the expense of maintaining this obligation (*8) as not *everybody* made the accustomed and expected 'donation' in return to the church. In later centuries, the Cistercians found difficulty in recruiting their lay-brothers, who complained of being given too much hard manual work to do and the loneliness spent on the outlying granges often at some distance from the abbey tending crops or sheep. The system had largely fallen into disuse even before the high death toll and ensuing rising demand and price of labour following the long famines, pestilence and plagues of the early to mid 14th Century.

The great abbeys - some of which grew into such profitable estates that their abbots lived in them in almost regal splendour - became rivals. Fountains Abbey in Yorkshire was also Cistercian, and was founded by the Cistercians and other monks leaving St Mary's Abbey in York in opposition to the sophisticated high-living and growing personal fortune of the Abbot there. Henry VIII ended it all; the great religious houses of England had suffered a steady decline due to Henry VIII's growing rift with the Pope and his threats to part company with Rome and found The Church of England, which finally happened in 1532. Rufford - although never especially wealthy in its possessions and deep in debt by then - was one of the first to be 'dissolved' in an atmosphere of charges of 'indecent and disgraceful offences against God' concerning the last abbot, made after a series of alleged love affairs by him involving married women. True or not, these charges led to the removal of the abbot from Rufford Abbey and it became the property of the Crown in 1536; various choice bits were 'removed' by Henry VIII's Commissioners and the site became almost derelict - it was finally given by Henry VIII as a gift to the Earl of Shrewsbury in 1537. 'Rufford Abbey' enjoyed a rebirth in the 17th century when it passed into the hands of first the Talbot family, and secondly the

Savile family, who added the large country house, lakes, landscaped parks and gardens that you see today and renewed the forestry where it had been cut down in the preceding two centuries.

The prosperity of both Rufford Abbey and nearby Newstead Abbey (founded by Henry II in 1172) was based on wool. A high grade wool cloth was woven from these fleeces throughout the York-Lincoln-Stamford area, named *Scarlet*. Lincoln was famed for producing this cloth, sometimes dyed red using 'grain', the name given by the English to the imported Mediteranean *kermes vermilio* insect husks (as they resembled grains of corn) from 'granet', the French word for them introduced by the Normans. However it was very expensive, and the duty on the finished product twice that of any other. Historical evidence that 'lincoln-green' may actually have been 'lincoln-grain' and hence bright red is interesting - two Victorian era painters chose to depict Robin Hood wearing bright red rather than dark green clothing (*9).

Pagan or pre-Christian images or ideals in the early Robin Hood stories were probably replaced by acceptable Christian ones. Parts of the Robin Hood legend bear more than a passing resemblance to The New Testament ; it is a John - but not The Baptist in the River Jordan - who gives Robin Hood the 'full immersion' rebirth, and the holy man who carries the young Robin Hood across the water is not St Christopher but The Curtal Friar. There are many similarities to indicate a past storyteller with his tongue firmly in cheek 'borrowing' ideas from Holy Scripture in the same way he adapted Greek and Roman texts - for example, the story of Odysseus at the end of his Odyssey long after the end of the Trojan Wars - using a bow only he could string, with which he then throws off his disguise and shoots his rivals dead - stands comparison with one of the old stories about 'Robin Hood'. There are probably lots more.

Footnotes

1. A heretic was burned at the stake after the judgement of a Church Court in London in 1210.
2. Southwell and its beautiful Minster is a day out in itself. An inspiring and beautifully kept example of Norman religious architecture, a visit there with a local guide to explore and see the 'pepperpot tops', 'Green Men', Roman relics, Thompson's Mouse,

Silver pennies circa AD 1205, found in Sherwood

the Eagle Lectern and many other aspects of great interest is highly recommended. A local circular walk is very popular.

3. King Stephen's eldest son Eustace was never acknowledged by the Pope as the legitimate heir and he forbade the clergy to do so based on Stephen's 'unlawful seizing' of the English crown. This - combined with Eustace's death in 1153 - led to the rival claim being powerfully supported by the Church.

4. 'The Curtal Friar' (the ancestor of the Friar Tuck character) was in the early Robin Hood ballad a former soldier who renounced his trade and lived as a hermit on charity. His religious beliefs however didn't stop him during his occupation of his hermitage defeating several visitors over seven years who having heard of his formidable military reputation decided to find out for themselves if it was true. A monk's habit was 'curtailed' by hoisting it up away from dirt or damp, and the 'tuck' which held it in place is the cord or rope worn around the waist.

5. Grimston village doesn't exist today, but the site of it is known and the area has given birth to some folklore and 'ghost' stories. The village probably disappeared through local depopulation through the establishment of Rufford Abbey, but in local folklore it sank during the earthquake of 1189. Undulations in the tarmac road surface that occurred here in the 1970's was explained by locals as 'Grimston village coming back up'. The uneven road surface was - rather disappointingly, I thought - found to be due to mining subsidence. Another earth tremor occurred here in 1999.

6. A *Cellarer* is featured in an old Robin Hood ballad. 'High-living' in the midst of the overall poverty of their flocks and congregations on the part of senior clergy became one of the main targets for admonition by Robin Hood and his band.

7. From an old term for the planet Venus when appearing as the 'Evenstar'.

8. Newstead Priory got into financial difficulties through

79

'The Curtal Friar'; still defending the hermitage at Foutaindale.

maintaining this traditional hospitality during the great famine of 1205. King John added Hucknall church and the watermeadows of Bestwood Park in 1206 to the monks holdings, but in 1295 Newstead once again was forced to ask the King to grant them a suspension of this hospitality and elect a manager to supervise the whole estate. Newstead was under Royal protection once again in 1310 after another great famine. A visit by the Court was a very expensive honour to be bestowed with.

9. You can see one of these paintings *'Robin Hood entertaining King Richard the Lionheart in Sherwood Forest'* by Daniel MacLise in Nottingham Castle Museum Art Gallery; *'Robin Hood and his Merry Men in Sherwood Forest'* is the other, by Warren Edward George.

A new and informative exhibition on the everyday life of a Cistercian monk is in the atmospheric old ruined lay-brothers 'frater' at Rufford Country Park.

Two monks were taken at Rufford Abbey by the Foresters of Sherwood in the 1200's for poaching deer in the forest; one was arrested for murdering one of the other monks in 1280 and another two brothers from here in 1307 were found guilty of highway robbery! A tall but ghostly black-robed monk is still said to haunt Rufford Abbey ruins; he does not like the fact that we can all now enjoy its splendour and has a habit of tapping visitors on the shoulder with a bony finger in an effort to get them to quickly move on! If that isn't enough, a freezing cold ghost-baby gets into bed with you and a 'White Lady' figure as at Newstead Abbey floats through the park. The Park also features a watermill, lakes and wildlife reserves, and many woodland walks. The Savile Restaurant serves meals, and a self-service snack bar stands by The Orangery. The Rufford Country Park Rangers stage many special events throughout the year. Admission to the Country Park is generally free except for special events, and there is a large car park for visitors.

The magnificent Norman architecture in Southwell Minster and its 'Green Men' in the Chapter House and choir should not be missed, and a visitor centre there offers a guidebook for both cathedral and village heritage trail around this outstanding historic building and its environs. A small admission charge is requested from visitors to help with the upkeep of the cathedral; after being spiritually fortified, an adjacent tea-room provides an excellent selection of refreshments and snacks to fortify you physically for the rest of your tour. Charles I finally surrendered to the opposing powers during the English Civil Wars and spent his last night of freedom at the nearby 'Saracens Head', which has atmospheric accommodation, a restaurant and bar for visitors.

Part Seven

Medieval Food and Drink

FOOD

Bread was the most important staple; but not the white wheaten bread we know today. That was only eaten by the wealthy, who owned all the best land capable of growing it. The commoners ate brown bread, rough barley and oats milled and ground including un-winnowed husk. At times of bad harvest, even bread made from peas, beans, or even beechnuts and acorns was consumed. The wealthy ate their meals from 'trenchers' instead of plates, being large flat loaves of barley bread; these were often collected after use and given to the poor as they held scraps and the residue of grease and fat from the meal, and used to thicken soup or broth. Bread was baked in towns and sold at market, but outlying villages baked their own. Town bakers were often looked upon with suspicion, due to rumours of them adding sawdust, floor sweepings, earth, sand and even plaster to the dough - the penalty for any baker caught doing this were severe. In 1267 an Assize of Bread was dictated, laying down the regulation sizes and weight of loaves for sale, and it also set the price for the finished loaf so poor people could expect to buy and get a reasonable and necessary daily product. To avoid any accusation of 'short weight' after this edict, bakers added an extra loaf to the traditional batch of twelve (the origin of the term 'a bakers dozen').

Pork, mutton and beef are all Norman-French words, and reflect the fact that meat was generally unknown to many common folk - the daily dinner was a thick soup or 'pottage' (*1) of vegetables such as peas, beans, carrots, turnips, onions or leeks, flavoured with herbs. Some pottage was so thick it could be sliced like bread when cool. Religious decrees also meant that even if meat *was* available, it couldn't be eaten on half the days of the year; especially Wednesdays, Fridays, Saturdays and the season of Lent through to Easter. These were 'fish days' when the eating of meat was forbidden; pickled or salted herring was common, brought into Nottinghamshire from the North Sea through Fiskerton, the port on the River Trent. 'Stockfish' (salted-down cod) was the only other generally available seafish - only folk by the sea or large inland rivers ate fresh seafish. These folk also enjoyed shellfish like mussels, shrimps, oysters and crabs. Freshwater rivers also held trout, bream, salmon, grayling and tench. These fish were often taken using nets, transported in barrels of water and used to regularly stock 'stews' or fishponds for breeding on the larger estates and abbeys to ensure a supply of fresh fish. Smaller fishponds also bred tasty carp for the wealthy and the larger ones held pike for the commoners.

Beavers were once common in rivers and streams in Sherwood, but they became extinct through being hunted for their meat as they were classed by the clergy as 'fish' as they lived in water and had a fishy-like tail; visiting geese were also classed as 'fish' and the excuse to eat them was it was thought they were born out at sea! The clergy were permitted to eat most 'two-legged' but not 'four-legged' meats - chicken and duck could be eaten by them whereas beef, pork, goat and sheep could not. Partridges, pheasants, swans, peacocks, quail, plovers, snipe and heron were also consumed - even larks, blackbirds and finches were served up as tasty side-dishes at clerical 'feasts'.

Red meat was generally pork, mutton or goat and almost the sole preserve of the wealthy classes. Beef was known, but it was quite rare on the dinner table except in winter after beasts were slaughtered when there was no grazing to feed them on, and most of the meat 'salted-down' for preservation. A future breeding-stock would be retained, as oxen and cattle formed the main draught-strength for pulling carts and ploughs; but they were expensive both to acquire and feed and hence quite few in number. The average size of livestock was also much smaller than today - for example, a full grown sheep then would pass for a lamb today. The innards of all these animals (known then as 'numbles', which gave rise to the term 'to eat humble pie') would be made into pies for the less well-off. Poultry such as ducks, pigeons and geese could be enjoyed by everyone - if you had any. Eggs were precious, and any birds were well guarded in coop, dovecote and hen-house whilst being fattened up. Dairy products (mostly goats milk and cheese) were available, but milk was considered as a drink fit only for children, the aged or the sick. The cream of any milk was skimmed off and reserved for the wealthy, the lower orders getting only skimmed milk. Cream cheese was served as an aside to the main 'top table' meal of roast meat. Skimmed milk cheese on the poor man's table was so hard it often required cutting with a saw or breaking up with a blunt instrument before it could be eaten; it did however provide much-need protein and did keep for an awfully long time!

Fruit was generally always cooked, as the raw fruit was regarded as harbouring 'disease'. Grapes grew over in Derbyshire in vineyards on the thinner soil - apples, pears, apricots, cherries and plums were common, grown and cultivated in settled and managed orchards as part of the estate. Raisins, dates, figs and prunes were imported from the Continent along with lemons and oranges, but their price dictated they were seen and eaten only by the very wealthy. Honey from managed beehives (*2) - used in making 'mead' (and its close relative, metheglyn, consumed like Port) - was the only sweetener, although sugar was becoming known after being brought back by Crusaders from the east but it didn't catch on due to the terrific expense of transportation from overseas until much later on; rice also became known at that time but was difficult to grow here. Spices from Europe and the Far East also returned with these voyagers and were popularly used to flavour salted meats - and probably disguise the taste of meat 'gone off' - but these too were fantastically expensive. The only spice imported in any quantity and hence within the scope of the commoner's purse in the Nottingham market place was Pepper.

Cooks and Stewards in wealthy households, some Abbeys and of course at Court could and did create from this wide variety of ingredients meals involving many courses or 'removes' all both tasty and pleasing to the eye. Poorer folk simply did the best they could with whatever was available in terms of their produce by adding nuts, fruit, wild herbs, fungi and a few plants to differ a largely monotonous daily diet - and 'poached' animals at every opportunity.

Footnotes
1. Simply the French word for 'soup'.
2. Honey bees were recorded by one monk as being *'God's little servants'*.

DRINK

Water, ale, cider, milk, and mead were the most common drinks available to commoners. Tea was as yet unknown, but 'tisanes' were made by infusing common herbs such as camomile, lemon balm, mint or toadflax in hot water to be drunk hot or later cold. Rich folk could drink imported foreign wines and spirits such as brandy. Each manor would have a 'buttery' and each village a 'brewhouse' for brewing and distilling alcohol for drinks, medicines and cosmetics. They also made country wines from orchard fruits, blackberries, elderflowers, elderberry and some vegetables.

Ale - sometimes referred to as 'beer' from the Anglo-Saxon *bere-legh'* or barley - was a malted brew using the grain, sometimes flavoured with herbs and each new brew of varying strengths was drunk in oceanic quantities within a short space of time as it would not keep (the preservative hop was not used in England at that time). Everyone brewed ale, from the manor landlords to the Church - after the harvest, an eagerly awaited beer drinking festival from the first of the new crop would take place; special brews commemorated weddings, funerals, religious feasts or holidays. The amount of salted meat eaten in winter also engendered beer-drinking in prodigious quantities, although any excuse at any time always led to a 'booze-up' (*1). Roadside taverns - often no more than wayside private dwellings or huts - would advertise a new brew of ale ready to drink by hanging a large green bush outside on a peg. Larger establishments in towns had rooms with beds, sold food and took in travellers. If it existed, the *Blue Boar Tavern* in Sherwood would have seen merchants, monks, foresters, pedlars, outlaws, soldiers and even some nobles coming from miles around forgetting their differences and dropping in to take a mug or two of the famous home-brewed strong 'Old October' ale whilst rubbing ambivalent shoulders with each other!

Footnote

1. A special brew was made for the wedding, named the 'Bride Ale' and the origin of the term *bridal* . Alcohol taken in large quantities has always been a sop for forgetting your troubles - albeit temporarily. You would pay for drink, food and other comestibles with the standard coin of the early Middle Ages, the silver penny. The silver pennies minted by Henry II in 1180 were used right

through to 1247, but by 1205 many of these coins had aroused suspicion through widespread 'clipping and shaving' and were melted down and re-issued by King John, showing his crowned head on them instead. The year 1205 saw more coins required as inflation spiralled due to food shortages after a prolonged famine. Twelve pennies equalled one shilling; twenty shillings made one pound. A lower means of exchange simply meant cutting a penny in half or quarters with shears, giving us the terms 'halfling' (halfpenny) and 'fourthing' (farthing). The 'mark' was a measure of continental monetary exchange, valued in England at thirteen shillings and fourpence (being two-thirds of a pound sterling) as an English pound sterling was worth four times a Normandy or Anjou pound. Anglo-Saxon peasants would often barter and exchange goods, but from 1066 the Normans insisted on their land-rents being paid in coin, and the old Anglo-Saxon 'food rent' system declined. In the late 12th century a skilled man such as a carpenter, mason or thatcher could earn two pennies per day when he could get work. Ale was priced at only a half-penny per gallon and by comparison, a silver penny could buy you two gallons of strong cider or three large loaves of barley bread. A pair of leather shoes would cost you three silver pennies, and a pair of good boots four pennies. Items involving metal of any sort were the most expensive to buy.

Part Eight

Medieval Medicine

In the early medieval era, if any of Robin Hood's 'Merry Men' fell ill it would be regarded in quite a different way from today. A knowledge of surgery and healing in the early days was looked on by the Church as potentially heretical (the church banned any form of human dissection for example) and was also likely to get you charged with witchcraft! Illnesses were seen to be a result of loss of balance in your diet, past sins, personal wickedness or in extreme cases, bewitchment or enchantment. The priest was equally important when seeking a cure as any doctor; and some remedies and cures were based on folklore, superstition and old wives tales, such as wearing talismans to ward off the 'evil eye'.

Some pretty nasty 'cures' were often worse than the illness, made from frogs and toads, snakes, ground up stones, precious jewels or even tablets of pure gold taken internally. Surgery or blood-letting in England was carried out by barbers as they were the only chaps trusted in close proximity with sharp knives! There were no anaesthetics except for strong drink and during a serious operation such as trepanning the skull 'to let the devil out' the patient would be secured by being tied down until they passed out in pain; the only antiseptic being a few herbal potions and onion or garlic.

Blood was generally held to be the most important aspect of the body; it was believed there were two kinds of blood which moved up and down the body in different directions, and both held four different 'humours' and affected life in different ways - a recommended cure was to open a vein in a particular place and let the 'bad blood' flow out (as in one ballad *The Death of Robin Hood*). Herbal lore, good food and careful nursing was the only kind likely to be of use to an already sick man; each village and religious house had its own herb-garden or 'herbarium' holding the nine 'sacred' herbs of vervain, lavender, rosemary, hellebore, wormwood, sage, comfrey and marjoram and such plants as sage, parsley and thyme would be grown not just for cooking but for healing too, and recently some have enjoyed a new popularity in use in complimentary medicine and aromatherapy still surrounded by past mystique and superstition. A few examples follow:

Sage; an all-rounder for liver, stomach, blood and nervous complaints
Garlic; for muscular strength
Valerian; for swollen joints and sprains
Mistletoe; for blood disorders
Coltsfoot; for coughs and bronchitis
Yarrow or white willow bark; for a curing a headache
Comfrey; for sprains or aches and pains
Vervain; to stop bleeding from a cut or after childbirth

There are many more. There were books on the subject of medicine and cooking but most were written in Greek or Latin and kept locked-up in the libraries of monasteries and so useless to the average peasant or villein, who couldn't read anyway. Most of their daily treatments came from the village 'wise woman' who held hereditary knowledge or perhaps a monk specialising in treatments and serving in the hospital at any of the nearby religious houses. Returning Crusaders brought back much 'modern' knowledge of surgery and the treatment of disease or wounds from the more enlightened East - most of which the Church here in England would not accept or permit.

A doctor extracts an arrowhead

Burnet-saxifrage can be used to treat kidney stones, and Ground-elder to treat gout and arthritis; both are common woodland plants and both are common complaints of the era. Hemlock looks very similar to both and if taken by mistake would lead to your instant death instead of a cure!

Anyone wishing to find out more about using wild plants and herbs will find plenty of material on library bookshelves to read; there are in addition some excellent entertaining, educational and informative weekend courses run by local Rangers on this aspect here in Bestwood Country Park. BUT - exercise extreme caution before conducting any experiment involving tasting or consuming any wild plant or fungi. Picking or digging-up wild plants or flowers is not permitted under The Wildlife and Countryside Act.

Part Nine

War and Peace

After 1066 and the Norman Conquest, both England and Normandy were still subject to unrest. Ireland, Wales and Scotland considered themselves independent from any Norman rule, and from 1071 a series of 'Saxon' revolts in Northern England had to be dealt with at the same time as a watch kept for a new Scandinavian invasion; back across the Channel, France had designs on invading Normandy. Local disagreements in both places would give rise to bloody skirmishing, and civil war also periodically raised its ugly head over the next five centuries, mostly due to disputed rights of succession to the throne being hotly contested between rivals. Between 1066 and 1500 England was continuously upset by foreign and civil wars, Crusades, border disputes, enemy invasions, battles, unrest, oppression, pestilence and brigandry. All these disputes called for military power in the form of soldiers.

The 'feudal' system tied a realm together by oath and homage by linking each man to the one 'above' him in a social contract by means of sworn fealty; using land ownership as the common bond and means of support (*1). The arrangement for men working the land to support the military, originally created during Anglo-Saxon times based on one senior fighting man - fully equipped and sometimes mounted - per five 'hides' (a measurement of land from an old Saxon term based on an area a man could plough in a single day to support a family, roughly120 acres), was developed and enhanced by the Normans after 1066. At a time of a major threat, the Crown could call out a 'levy' of every man of military age (between sixteen and sixty-five) from a shire or county to support the nobles and their semi-professional armed retinues to defend the realm bringing any weapon they could get their hands on (*2). It was calculated as seen that the nobles' holdings could and should support a number of trained soldiers, to be brought to war armed and equipped from the revenue of the estate, to support those already retained on a permanent basis. In cases of less dire necessity such as a local revolt, pirate raid or an expansion of the

Stringing the bow

kingdom by invasion spearheaded by the Kings 'household' troops, the Crown could call on the nobles holding land anywhere for military service, bringing a fixed number of armed and trained men with them based on the size of the lands held ; an average gives around 7000 knights available for service in total, serving between forty and sixty days based on their 'knights fees' of an income averaging £20 per annum. The size of these retinues rose and fell with the need to maintain them; in peacetime they would still require paying and feeding and be subject to a loss of efficiency through boredom. Some proven and loyal 'vassals' were given allocations of land to support them 'off-duty'. Any shortfall in soldiers due to their absence on Crusade from 1096-1210 could be filled by training extra men if there was time, and if not by hiring mercenaries; but these did not give the same loyal service and could - as King John discovered - change sides or just go home if things went wrong or the money ran out.

Theoretically, the system would enable skilled full-time fighting men to defend the civilians, who supported them in return with food and shelter. Some very ambitious, rich and powerful nobles used the system to set themselves up with small personal armies to pursue their own ends, settle an old score with a rival or browbeat a rival neighbour into submission, particularly during times of civil war and although prohibited to do so by the King. Holdings and crops would be burned, villages ransacked, their occupants killed and the livestock run off. Small but powerful professional mercenary forces raised on a short-term basis and paid for in cash, land or booty could form or re-inforce armies, hold territory or conquer neighbouring areas; a tactic used by the experienced commander Duke William of Normandy in 1066 to invade England (*3) and by King John in 1216 to try to crush his Baron's revolt after he repudiated *Magna Carta* (*4). This set the growing precedent in later centuries when powerful barons allied with each other to feather their own nests and make or break Kings.

Tournaments were made legal by Richard I in 1194, who saw an outlet there for men with his warlike spirits. Under special conditions with a licence from the King, a combatant paid his entrance fee to take part in the contest at one of the five 'tilting grounds' where the ensuing 'sport' often became a serious brawl, leading to injury and even death. Defeat at the tourney at the hands of a fellow knight could include the loss of your horse, armour and the rest of your gear as he could claim them as a reward. Some knights became almost 'professional' - travelling from one tourney to the next, scrutinising the 'league-tables' of fellow tourney-knights.

The castles built in England from AD1068 would also have to be garrisoned by knights in current service and held by foot soldiers (in varying numbers as the climate of war rose and fell) under a loyal 'Constable' appointed by the King himself. The county would be headed by the King's personal representative - the Sheriff - and in wartime the county Sheriff's and castle Constable's would work closely together in raising and directing any county 'levy'. In peacetime AD1200, Nottingham Castle probably held a number of knights and around twenty to thirty soldiers, administrators and officials, with a steward overseeing the logisitical aspects of cooks, servants, brewers, butchers and bakers, all under the overall supervision of the Constable. The garrison would exercise in drill, train with personal arms, learn to handle siege equipment such as catapults and heavy crossbows, and maintain the gear and equipment in storage in the armoury. Any revolt or disturbance in the town that was too much for the Nottingham Town Watch to handle would see the garrison guard turned out to help them break a few heads if necessary to re-establish order. Any public punishment resulting from such a revolt would be closely supervised by soldiers too. For public appearances in any climate of unrest, the Constable would provide the Sheriff with an powerful armed guard of men to protect him from any demonstration of public opinion getting *too* close.

A *Commission of Array* - as specified in 1258 by Henry III - made sure that each landowner in each County fulfilled their obligations. In that year, smaller landowners (those holding lands worth £2 or more per annum in revenue) were required to 'serve as, or provide' an archer for the Array to support the 'horse and foot'. Archers were cheaper and easier to equip than trained and armoured foot-soldiers, even if their rate of pay for service was higher (*5) but in earlier days couldn't be expected or risked in a hand-to-hand fight in pitched battles. County Commissioners attended statutory practice sessions decreed by law where men would be called on and encouraged to practice their military skills, including archery. Sundays would see men with bows - not necessarily 'longbows' - all over England shooting at targets and the 'clout' in woodland clearings and on village commons. From 1250, archers - after the surprises they inflicted as 'commoners' against opposing soldiers in the early Welsh and Scots Wars - began to approach the point where they were considered highly important in the formation of English armies by the end of the century. In the initial form of semi-irregular bodies of close to medium-range deadly 'artillery support' for the infantry and Horse, in later centuries they developed into regular household companies, by then semi-armoured and using the more powerful and longer-ranging 'English' longbow and used not just in their traditional 'artillery' role but also as troops in assaults on enemy fortifications.

This large body of men in England trained in varying degrees to warfare far outstripped that in any other European country; most military forces there were small, permanently retained professional and aristocratic bodies of well-armoured knights and companies of foot. The confident companies of partly armoured infantry and archers using the powerful 'standardised' longbow as part of the English county levy under a stout captain laid the foundations for famous victories such as Crecy (1346), Poitiers (1356) and Agincourt (1415).

Many minor skirmishes and battles were fought in and around Nottinghamshire throughout The Dark Ages period such as Hatfield (632), Trent and Nottingham (868 and 1015); battles of 'The Middle Ages' include Northallerton (1138), Lincoln (1141), Evesham (1265), Borobridge (1322), Bosworth (1485) and East Stoke (1487).

Footnotes

1. Although Robin Hood uses the growing precedent set by William I and asserted by Henry III that a man's main fealty was always to the King rather than his immediate lord. Under the growing institutionalised royal despotism post-1086, the only way to change a rapacious, weak or foolhardy Kings' will was to break your oath to him and rebel, try to bring him to terms or simply overthrow him and crown someone else to rule instead.

2. The 'fyrd' in Anglo-Saxon England or the *arriere-ban* in Normandy, an emergency but indifferently armed militia to support the main body of fighting men. Harold called it out in 1066 to support his housecarles and their 'select fyrdsmen' fight the invasion of his brother Tostig and Harald Hardrada at Stamford Bridge, then marched them south to fight Duke William coming ashore from Normandy near Hastings. Weapons reflected their mainly agricultural origins and included hayforks, clubs, flails, scythes and billhooks. John I, with the threat of French Invasion, in 1205 re-organised the fyrd using as a basis The Assize of Arms of 1181.

3. Duke William, nicknamed 'The Bastard' - a tough, relentless, rapacious and ruthless soldier who never learned to read or write, descended from Viking raiders who settled in Northern France and whose parents never married - was under pressure from the age of seven (when his father The Duke of Normandy died unexpectedly on a pilgrimage in 1035) from both neighbouring French rulers and rivals threatening to invade Normandy. William had to pay large

sums to both support and create armies of soldiers to help him defend his lands. William through Robert II had a hereditary claim to the English Crown since 1002, reinforced by Edward the Confessor in 1051 and known to Harold Godwinson, already under the influence of Normandy. The claim made for Duke William by the powerful Norman clergy that Earl Harold in accepting the English Crown in 1066 had betrayed and usurped the rightful heir (Duke William) got support from the Pope and rallied many Normans with 'God was On their Side' calling for a rightful and just campaign, William had cause to fear a French invasion from the east as he left Normandy to the west - despite some strong frontier defences - and had to hire mercenaries to pursue his claim with promises of bonuses in the form of land or plunder if successful. After 1066, his nickname changed to 'The Conqueror'; during a campaign in northern England, William punished the revolt of 1076 by utterly devastating a swathe of land, including burning York and killing hundreds of people, right up to Durham. In 1079 back in Normandy he was unhorsed and defeated during a family feud by his son Robert; still battling on at the age of 59, he was accidentally thrown from his horse during the siege of Mantes in 1087 and died from the internal injuries sustained. Robert got Normandy, William 'Rufus' was given the throne of England, Henry got most of his father's money (William's eldest son, Richard, was dead, killed when he fell from his horse hunting in the New Forest). Duke William's favourite oath was *'Splendour of God!'* although at times he very probably said far worse than that. Although The Conqueror's funeral was disgraced through a series of events and family squabbles and interred at Caen without dignity, William I remained a legendary figure throughout the medieval period, and many a nobleman's idea of an ideal 'role model', leading to them becoming the kind of feudal gangster Robin Hood is often called upon to chastise - in the movies, anyway!

4. King John hired many foreign mercenaries and oficials to support him during his reign, and he made a lot of enemies by doing so. *Magna Carta* banned carrying the crossbow as King John saw it as the weapon of assassins; his elder brother King Richard I 'the Lionheart' was killed by a shot from one in France. On 26th April 1199 during a siege at Chalus in France, a crossbowman named Peter Basilius shot an English crossbow bolt

back at the beseigers, which struck Richard in the neck. Richard broke off the shaft and continued with the seige. However the delay in removing the head caused blood poisoning and Richard fell mortally ill. Richard forgave Basilius before dying, but after Richard's death Basilius was tortured and executed. In Robin Hood films (including *Men in Tights*) you often note 'baddies' are traditionally equipped with crossbows as opposed to the 'goodies' who use longbows.

5. Henry I had - as part of his military household - a full-time unit of archers as early as AD1114, who may have been Welshmen. From the 11th to the late 13th Centuries, it was much more usual to find crossbowmen fulfilling this role. Expensive to create and train, mercenary companies of continental crossbowmen could be 'hired' short-term to strengthen or support any infantry and cavalry force. The word 'archer' comes from the Norman French word for a bow - *'archet'*. In Saxon England prior to the Conquest anyone using a bow would be referred to as a 'bowman'.

Part Ten

" Fare Ye Well! "

The Saxon nobleman Waltheof - who William I executed after the rebellions of 1071- 1076 was 'The Earl of Huntingdon'. There are even earlier tantalising clues used in speculation, but most of the 'hard' evidence used by historians in the past to support a case for a *real* Robert or Robin Hood falls into the period between 1226 and 1354 (Henry III to Edward III).

The tax system, legal system and coinage of Anglo-Saxon England were all inherited and *not* instituted by the Normans in 1066 - the 'common law' then in existence was later widely adapted by the Normans to suit the changing circumstances. Before then it catered for all but was wide open to re-interpretation and abuse by the Norman clerks and officials who replaced the Saxon post-holders and the 'aristocrats' who cruelly enforced it after 1068 in the face of pending overseas invasion, Saxon rebellions and peasant insurrection.

Feature films and television have gone some way away from the early beginnings of our hero, but I think the values he stands for today are more widely appreciated than ever before. Robin Hood is usually identified on television and in cinema as a chap from a noble background standing up to unjust authority in the 12th Century from the consequences of the single most important radical change in our history after the Roman Invasion - the Norman Conquest. This event didn't happen overnight but it must have seemed that way to our ancestors looking back over the preceding 'Dark Ages' and the creeping Danelaw and Viking occupations, which were both neither total nor permanent, and the English Crown did have strong ties with Normandy from before the 10th Century ("Halley's Comet" - as we now know it - in 1066 was seen as a sign from God and the portent of this great and imminent change). Poor old Prince/King John comes in for a lot of criticism; but Richard I 'The Lionheart' was not the benevolent King he is 'traditionally' held to be - history books show he was a ruthless soldier, no friend to the Church, and rarely in England. He used England as a 'money pot', established the strict taxation often attributed to his younger brother and is supposed to have said that he would have sold London if he could ever have found anyone able to afford to buy it. Robin Hood was 'traditionally' still around during the signing of *Magna Carta* by King John in 1215 but storytellers both old and modern are strangely quiet on this subject - but isn't it what it contains what Robin Hood was fighting for? In the oldest published ballads and stories Robin Hood is mentioned as operating in Barnsdale and Sherwood during the reigns of 'Henry' or 'Edward' - not 'Richard' or 'John'.

A man named Robert Hode was outlawed in York in 1225 for not appearing at court; another Robert Hode is mentioned as being cited for murder in Cirencester in 1213. By 1262 the surname 'Robynhood' had appeared and was first recorded in a Berkshire court case where a man ('William, son of Robert the Smith) ran off and was 'outlawed'. In the poem Piers Plowman by William Langland written in 1377 mention is made of 'rymes of Robin Hood and Randolph, Earl of Chester' (the Earl was active between 1181 and 1232).

The tradition of Robin Hood fighting against Prince John's oppression whilst King Richard the Lion heart is away on Crusade and later imprisoned in Austria originates in 1521 with John Major's 'History of Britain', and became the accepted norm after *Ivanhoe*, the highly successful novel by Sir Walter Scott, published in 1820. Before they year 1400 historians only disputed the historical era of Robin Hood ; only after the year 1600 did they began to doubt his existence.

I think 'Robin Hood' both in myth and legend originates *much* further back than all of these. Neanderthal, Cro-Magnon, Celt, Greek, Roman, Angle, Saxon, Dane and Viking all brought stories and sagas with them to this land featuring characters who can be compared with an embryonic outlaw hero like Robin Hood ; in a similar way the story of Robin Hood impressed J M Barrie so much on his visit to Nottingham it led to him writing the childrens classic, *Peter Pan*.

When the local greenbelt here in Nottinghamshire at Hucknall, Bestwood and Kirkby was threatened, one of the letters in opposition to modern development received by the inquiry was said to be from 'Robin Hood, Maid Marian and Friar Tuck'; the ensuing public demonstrations before the authorities inquiry saw a host of modern Robin-Hood's concerned with preservation and conservation aspects turning out to defend the countryside and their 'rights'. Following claims and opinions from other surrounding counties, a degree of debate has ensued when they lay claim to Robin Hood as 'theirs', causing a flurry amongst Nottingtonians before they dim and blur. The amount of historical data supporting these different opinions found by modern Robin-hunters increases yearly; but I still firmly believe he belongs to each and every one of Us, and is beyond any provincial or national boundary. Robin Hood has constantly evolved before and even since being set down on paper for us just before 1500; he has changed his status, his looks, his behaviour and even his name. He has served as a role model for several other heroic fictional figures; although unacknowledged the comparisons are eventually made. The reason he has evolved is that he has kept pace and faith with us, his creators. We have made him what he is, from demands arising from changes in social, economic and political aspects right down to and including the present day. He is cast in our image - or how we would wish it to be - in Robin Hood there is a little part of us all, and consequently in us all a little bit of Robin Hood. You can still find him if you look hard enough : you can see the reflection of Robin Hood in the eyes of hundreds of people you pass every day in the street. He is immortal as we are; he has given his name to some of the finest qualities and aspirations that human beings possess - hope, love, sharing, charity, self-sacrifice, immortality - and above all ... *freedom.* God Forbid we should all ever have to fight for our freedom as Robin Hood did; but many of our ancestors had to, and we should never forget the sacrifices they all made.

The motto of the City of Nottingham is *"Virtue lives on after Death".* Robin Hood is alive and well there and in Sherwood Forest - and many other places. In the night sky you can sometimes see Robin Hood's longbow bent ready to shoot; you will sometimes even see arrows from it streaking through the evening sky. I believe in the spirit of Robin Hood because I've seen the old traits traditionally attached to his arch-enemy the 'Sheriff of Nottingham' plenty of times! There is a lot of magic still in Sherwood Forest; I hope you continue 'on the outlaw trail' when you go back home from it and find out some more about Robin Hood from your local library or bookshop.

I leave you with this local rhyme ......

**IN SHERWOOD FOREST HAVE NO FEAR -
FOR IN ENGLAND'S DEEPEST DARKEST WOOD,
YOU CAN TODAY STILL FEEL AND HEAR
.... THE GHOST OF ROBIN HOOD !**

Useful Contacts

**The "On the Outlaw Trail" tour of Nottinghamshire and
"Robin Hood's Sherwood Forest" are both based on this
publication and the book
'The Legend of Robin Hood' by Richard Rutherford-Moore
(Capall Bann Publishing, ISBN 186163069-7)**

'On the Outlaw Trail' in Nottinghamshire and Sherwood Forest;
intimate guided tours to suit you seeing many sites associated with
Robin Hood in the company of the author as 'Blacke Dickon,
Forester of Sherwood AD1200' are available with no size or time
parameters for visitors to the shire or local school parties
(telephone 0115 - 9679926).

The author appears throughout the year at various events in
Sherwood Forest. The 'Robin Hood Festival' is held annually
around the Sherwood Forest Visitor Centre, Edwinstowe featuring
entertainment such as period archery displays and 'have-a-go-
yourself', jousting, plays, knightly combats, music and song - and
of course, outlaws and Nottingham soldiers. Telephone 01623
823202 for details of this and other events and attractions. The
'Robin Hood Pageant' is held at Nottingham Castle later in the
year.

You can also e-mail the Author of this publication on
r@armor.demon.co.uk

For more information or brochures on future attractions and
events in the area Nottinghamshire Tourist Unit (telephone 01623
822944, Ext. 220) or Nottingham City Information Desk (telephone
0115 - 9155330).

FREE DETAILED CATALOGUE

Capall Bann is owned and run by people actively involved in many of the areas in which we publish. A detailed illustrated catalogue is available on request, SAE or International Postal Coupon appreciated. **Titles can be ordered direct from Capall Bann, post free in the UK** (cheque or PO with order) or from good bookshops and specialist outlets.

Do contact us for details on the latest releases at: **Capall Bann Publishing, Freshfields, Chieveley, Berks, RG20 8TF.** Titles include:

A Breath Behind Time, Terri Hector
Angels and Goddesses - Celtic Christianity & Paganism, M. Howard
Arthur - The Legend Unveiled, C Johnson & E Lung
Astrology The Inner Eye - A Guide in Everyday Language, E Smith
Auguries and Omens - The Magical Lore of Birds, Yvonne Aburrow
Asyniur - Womens Mysteries in the Northern Tradition, S McGrath
Beginnings - Geomancy, Builder's Rites & Electional Astrology in the
       European Tradition, Nigel Pennick
Between Earth and Sky, Julia Day
Book of the Veil , Peter Paddon
Caer Sidhe - Celtic Astrology and Astronomy, Vol 1, Michael Bayley
Caer Sidhe - Celtic Astrology and Astronomy, Vol 2 M Bayley
Call of the Horned Piper, Nigel Jackson
Cat's Company, Ann Walker
Celtic Faery Shamanism, Catrin James
Celtic Faery Shamanism - The Wisdom of the Otherworld, Catrin James
Celtic Lore & Druidic Ritual, Rhiannon Ryall
Celtic Sacrifice - Pre Christian Ritual & Religion, Marion Pearce
Celtic Saints and the Glastonbury Zodiac, Mary Caine
Circle and the Square, Jack Gale
Compleat Vampyre - The Vampyre Shaman, Nigel Jackson
Creating Form From the Mist - The Wisdom of Women in Celtic Myth and
       Culture, Lynne Sinclair-Wood
Crystal Clear - A Guide to Quartz Crystal, Jennifer Dent
Crystal Doorways, Simon & Sue Lilly
Crossing the Borderlines - Guising, Masking & Ritual Animal Disguise in the
       European Tradition, Nigel Pennick
Dragons of the West, Nigel Pennick
Earth Dance - A Year of Pagan Rituals, Jan Brodie
Earth Harmony - Places of Power, Holiness & Healing, Nigel Pennick
Earth Magic, Margaret McArthur
Eildon Tree (The) Romany Language & Lore, Michael Hoadley

Enchanted Forest - The Magical Lore of Trees, Yvonne Aburrow
Eternal Priestess, Sage Weston
Eternally Yours Faithfully, Roy Radford & Evelyn Gregory
Everything You Always Wanted To Know About Your Body, But So Far
    Nobody's Been Able To Tell You, Chris Thomas & D Baker
Face of the Deep - Healing Body & Soul, Penny Allen
Fairies in the Irish Tradition, Molly Gowen
Familiars - Animal Powers of Britain, Anna Franklin
Fool's First Steps, (The) Chris Thomas
Forest Paths - Tree Divination, Brian Harrison, Ill. S. Rouse
From Past to Future Life, Dr Roger Webber
Gardening For Wildlife Ron Wilson
God Year, The, Nigel Pennick & Helen Field
Goddess on the Cross, Dr George Young
Goddess Year, The, Nigel Pennick & Helen Field
Goddesses, Guardians & Groves, Jack Gale
Handbook For Pagan Healers, Liz Joan
Handbook of Fairies, Ronan Coghlan
Healing Book, The, Chris Thomas and Diane Baker
Healing Homes, Jennifer Dent
Healing Journeys, Paul Williamson
Healing Stones, Sue Philips
Herb Craft - Shamanic & Ritual Use of Herbs, Lavender & Franklin
Hidden Heritage - Exploring Ancient Essex, Terry Johnson
Hub of the Wheel, Skytoucher
In Search of Herne the Hunter, Eric Fitch
Inner Celtia, Alan Richardson & David Annwn
Inner Mysteries of the Goths, Nigel Pennick
Inner Space Workbook - Develop Thru Tarot, C Summers & J Vayne
Intuitive Journey, Ann Walker Isis - African Queen, Akkadia Ford
Journey Home, The, Chris Thomas
Kecks, Keddles & Kesh - Celtic Lang & The Cog Almanac, Bayley
Language of the Psycards, Berenice
Legend of Robin Hood, The, Richard Rutherford-Moore
Lid Off the Cauldron, Patricia Crowther
Light From the Shadows - Modern Traditional Witchcraft, Gwyn
Living Tarot, Ann Walker
Lore of the Sacred Horse, Marion Davies
Lost Lands & Sunken Cities (2nd ed.), Nigel Pennick
Magic of Herbs - A Complete Home Herbal, Rhiannon Ryall
Magical Guardians - Exploring the Spirit and Nature of Trees, Philip Heselton
Magical History of the Horse, Janet Farrar & Virginia Russell
Magical Lore of Animals, Yvonne Aburrow
Magical Lore of Cats, Marion Davies
Magical Lore of Herbs, Marion Davies
Magick Without Peers, Ariadne Rainbird & David Rankine
Masks of Misrule - Horned God & His Cult in Europe, Nigel Jackson

104

Medicine For The Coming Age, Lisa Sand MD
Medium Rare - Reminiscences of a Clairvoyant, Muriel Renard
Menopausal Woman on the Run, Jaki da Costa
Mind Massage - 60 Creative Visualisations, Marlene Maundrill
Mirrors of Magic - Evoking the Spirit of the Dewponds, P Heselton
Moon Mysteries, Jan Brodie
Mysteries of the Runes, Michael Howard
Mystic Life of Animals, Ann Walker
New Celtic Oracle The, Nigel Pennick & Nigel Jackson
Oracle of Geomancy, Nigel Pennick
Pagan Feasts - Seasonal Food for the 8 Festivals, Franklin & Phillips
Patchwork of Magic - Living in a Pagan World, Julia Day
Pathworking - A Practical Book of Guided Meditations, Pete Jennings
Personal Power, Anna Franklin
Pickingill Papers - The Origins of Gardnerian Wicca, Bill Liddell
Pillars of Tubal Cain, Nigel Jackson
Places of Pilgrimage and Healing, Adrian Cooper
Practical Divining, Richard Foord
Practical Meditation, Steve Hounsome
Practical Spirituality, Steve Hounsome
Psychic Self Defence - Real Solutions, Jan Brodie
Real Fairies, David Tame
Reality - How It Works & Why It Mostly Doesn't, Rik Dent
Romany Tapestry, Michael Houghton
Runic Astrology, Nigel Pennick
Sacred Animals, Gordon MacLellan
Sacred Celtic Animals, Marion Davies, Ill. Simon Rouse
Sacred Dorset - On the Path of the Dragon, Peter Knight
Sacred Grove - The Mysteries of the Forest, Yvonne Aburrow
Sacred Geometry, Nigel Pennick
Sacred Nature, Ancient Wisdom & Modern Meanings, A Cooper
Sacred Ring - Pagan Origins of British Folk Festivals, M. Howard
Season of Sorcery - On Becoming a Wisewoman, Poppy Palin
Seasonal Magic - Diary of a Village Witch, Paddy Slade
Secret Places of the Goddess, Philip Heselton
Secret Signs & Sigils, Nigel Pennick
Self Enlightenment, Mayan O'Brien
Spirits of the Air, Jaq D Hawkins
Spirits of the Earth, Jaq D Hawkins
Spirits of the Water, Jaq D Hawkins
Spirits of the Fire, Jaq D Hawkins
Spirits of the Aether, Jaq D Hawkins
Stony Gaze, Investigating Celtic Heads John Billingsley
Stumbling Through the Undergrowth , Mark Kirwan-Heyhoe
Subterranean Kingdom, The, revised 2nd ed, Nigel Pennick
Symbols of Ancient Gods, Rhiannon Ryall
Talking to the Earth, Gordon MacLellan

Taming the Wolf - Full Moon Meditations, Steve Hounsome
Teachings of the Wisewomen, Rhiannon Ryall
The Other Kingdoms Speak, Helena Hawley
Tree: Essence of Healing, Simon & Sue Lilly
Tree: Essence, Spirit & Teacher, Simon & Sue Lilly
Through the Veil, Peter Paddon
Torch and the Spear, Patrick Regan
Understanding Chaos Magic, Jaq D Hawkins
Vortex - The End of History, Mary Russell
Warp and Weft - In Search of the I-Ching, William de Fancourt
Warriors at the Edge of Time, Jan Fry
Water Witches, Tony Steele
Way of the Magus, Michael Howard
Weaving a Web of Magic, Rhiannon Ryall
West Country Wicca, Rhiannon Ryall
Wildwitch - The Craft of the Natural Psychic, Poppy Palin
Wildwood King , Philip Kane
Witches of Oz, Matthew & Julia Philips
Wondrous Land - The Faery Faith of Ireland by Dr Kay Mullin
Working With the Merlin, Geoff Hughes
Your Talking Pet, Ann Walker

FREE detailed catalogue and FREE 'Inspiration' magazine

Contact: Capall Bann Publishing, Freshfields, Chieveley, Berks, RG20 8TF